Robert Smith and Co.

The General School Laws of Michigan

With Appendixes Compiled at the Office of the Superintendent of Public Instruction

Robert Smith and Co.

The General School Laws of Michigan
With Appendixes Compiled at the Office of the Superintendent of Public Instruction

ISBN/EAN: 9783337232375

Printed in Europe, USA, Canada, Australia, Japan

Cover: Foto ©Suzi / pixelio.de

More available books at **www.hansebooks.com**

THE
GENERAL SCHOOL LAWS

OF

MICHIGAN

WITH

APPENDIXES

COMPILED AT THE OFFICE OF THE

SUPERINTENDENT OF PUBLIC INSTRUCTION

1895

BY AUTHORITY

LANSING
ROBERT SMITH & CO., STATE PRINTERS AND BINDERS
1895

THIS VOLUME IS STATE PROPERTY.

CONTENTS.

4   CONTENTS.

APPENDIXES.

INTRODUCTORY.

Heretofore it has been the custom to publish an edition of the general school laws every fourth year, but the demand this year for a complete compilation which shall contain all the new school laws enacted and amendments made by the legislature of 1895, seems to warrant the issuing of an edition this year. In preparing it the arrangement in the edition of 1893 has been retained as far as practicable, in order that references to each edition may correspond as to chapter and section. This arrangement is followed strictly to chapter XX, which chapter is the new law for the compulsory education of children. But this law takes the place of chapters XX, XXI, and XXII of the school laws of 1893, and appears here as chapters XX, while the next chapter is number XXIII. Therefore the five chapters following chapter XX bear the same number as in the edition of 1893, the numbers of these chapters in the two editions thus remaining the same. Chapters XXIX, XXX, and XXXI are new laws which have taken effect during the year 1895. I desire to call the attention of school officers to all of the changes and additions made by the last legislature, and refer to them in their order as published in the book.

1. Amendment to section 17, page 16—qualifications of voters at school meetings.
2. Amendment to section 18, page 16—oath required of challenged voter.
3. Amendment to the eleventh paragraph of section 27, page 18—minimum number of months in school year raised from three to five.
4. Amendment to section 19, page 24—regulating the rate of tuition of non-resident pupils, and providing for the admission to school of children cared for at county houses.
5. Amendment to the sixth paragraph of section 21, page 25—defining what are necessary appendages to a schoolhouse.
6. Section 20, page 33—repealed by the tax law of 1893.

7. Amendment to section 11, page 48—proviso omitted.

8. Amendments to sections 1, 3, 4, 5, 11, and 13, of chapter 12—educational qualification of examiner, fixing dates for public examination of teachers, citizenship qualification of teachers, and qualification of city teachers.

9. Amendment to section 15, page 63—indorsement of certificates granted in other states.

10. Chapter XX—new law for the compulsory education of children.

11. Amendment to section 1, page 68—truancy.

12. Chapter XXIX—new law for teaching prevention of contagious diseases.

13. Chapter XXX—new law providing for examination for admission to the Agricultural College.

14. Chapter XXXI—new law authorizing the purchase of United States flags.

The digest of Supreme Court decisions embodied in appendix "A" has been brought up to date and the index carefully revised.

HENRY R. PATTENGILL,

Superintendent of Public Instruction.

GENERAL

SCHOOL LAWS OF MICHIGAN.

CONSTITUTIONAL PROVISIONS.

ARTICLE VIII.

STATE OFFICERS.

SECTION 1. There shall be elected at each biennial elec- State officers to tion, a Secretary of State, a Superintendent of Public be elected. Instruction, a State Treasurer, Commissioner of the Land Office, an Auditor General, and an Attorney General, for the term of two years. They shall keep their offices at Where to keep the seat of government, and shall perform such duties as offices. may be prescribed by law.

SEC. 2. Their term of office shall commence on the Term of office. first day of January, one thousand eight hundred and fifty-three, and of every second year thereafter.

SEC. 3. Whenever a vacancy shall occur in any of the Vacancy, how State offices, the Governor shall fill the same by appoint- filled. ment, by and with the advice and consent of the Senate, if in session.

ARTICLE XIII.

EDUCATION.

SECTION 1. The Superintendent of Public Instruction Duties of Super- shall have the general supervision of public instruction, intendent of Public Instruc- and his duties shall be prescribed by law. tion.

SEC. 2. The proceeds from the sales of all lands that School fund. have been or hereafter may be granted by the United States to the State for educational purposes, and the proceeds of all lands or other property given by individuals or appropriated by the State for like purposes, shall be and remain a perpetual fund, the interest and income of which, together with the rents of all such lands as may remain unsold, shall be inviolably appropriated and annually applied to the specific objects of the original gift, grant, or appropriation.

Escheats. SEC. 3. All lands, the titles to which shall fail from a defect of heirs, shall escheat to the State; and the interest on the clear proceeds from the sales thereof shall be appropriated exclusively to the support of primary schools.

Free schools. SEC. 4. The Legislature shall, within five years from the adoption of this constitution, provide for and establish a system of primary schools, whereby a school shall be kept without charge for tuition, at least three months **Instruction conducted in English language.** in each year, in every school district in the State; and all instruction in said schools shall be conducted in the English language.

District schools. When deprived of public money. SEC. 5. A school shall be maintained in each school district at least three months in each year. Any school district neglecting to maintain such school shall be deprived for the ensuing year of its porportion of the income of the primary school fund, and of all funds arising from taxes for the support of schools.

Election of Regents of the University. SEC. 6. There shall be elected in the year eighteen hundred and sixty-three, at the time of the election of a Justice of the Supreme Court, eight Regents of the University, two of whom shall hold their office for two years, two for four years, two for six years, and two for eight years. They shall enter upon the duties of their office on the first of January next succeeding their election. At every regular election of a Justice of the Supreme Court thereafter, there shall be elected two Regents, whose terms **Vacancy, how filled.** of office shall be eight years. When a vacancy shall occur in the office of Regent, it shall be filled by appointment of the Governor. The Regents thus elected shall constitute . the Board of Regents of the University of Michigan.

Regents a body corporate. SEC. 7. The Regents of the University, and their successors in office, shall continue to constitute the body corporate known by the name and title of "The Regents of the University of Michigan."

President of the University. SEC. 8. The Regents of the University shall, at their first annual meeting. or as soon thereafter as may be, elect a president of the University, who shall be *ex officio* a member of their board, with the privilege of speaking, but not of voting. He shall preside at the meetings of the Regents, and be the principal executive officer of the **University interest fund.** University. The Board of Regents shall have the general supervision of the University, and the direction and control of all expenditures from the University interest fund.

State Board of Education. SEC. 9. There shall be elected at the general election in the year one thousand eight hundred and fifty-two,

---

The minimum number of months to be taught was raised to five months by Legislature of 1895. See Act No. 15, Laws of 1895—¶ 11, Compiler's section No. 27.

three members of a State Board of Education; one for two years, one for four years, and one for six years; and at each succeeding biennial election there shall be elected one member of such board, who shall hold his office for six years. The Superintendent of Public Instruction shall *Superintendent of Public Instruction a member.* be *ex officio* a member and secretary of such board. The board shall have the general supervision of the State Normal School, and their duties shall be prescribed by *Care of normal school.* law.

SEC. 10. Institutions for the benefit of those inhabitants *Asylums.* who are deaf, dumb, blind, or insane, shall always be fostered and supported.

SEC. 11. The Legislature shall encourage the promotion *Agricultural school.* of intellectual, scientific, and agricultural improvement; and shall, as soon as practicable, provide for the establishment of an agricultural school. The Legislature may appropriate the twenty-two sections of salt spring lands now unappropriated, or the money arising from the sale of the same, where such lands have been already sold, and any land which may hereafter be granted or appropriated for such purpose, for the support and maintenance of such school, and may make the same a branch of the University, for instruction in agriculture and the natural sciences connected therewith, and place the same under the supervision of the Regents of the University.

SEC. 12. The Legislature shall also provide for the *Libraries.* establishment of at least one library in each township and city; and all fines assessed and collected in the sev- *Penal fines to be applied for libraries.* eral counties and townships for any breach of the penal laws, shall be exclusively applied to the support of such libraries, unless otherwise ordered by the township board of any township or the board of education of any city: *Proviso.* *Provided,* That in no case shall such fines be used for other than library or school purposes.

ARTICLE XIV.

FINANCE AND TAXATION.

SECTION 1. All specific State taxes, except those received *Specific taxes.* from the mining companies of the upper peninsula, shall be applied in paying the interest upon the primary school, university, and other educational funds, and the interest and principal of the State debt, in the order herein recited, until the extinguishment of the State debt, other than the amounts due to educational funds, when such specific taxes shall be added to and constitute a part of the primary school interest fund. The Legislature shall provide *Tax for state expenses.* for an annual tax, sufficient with other resources, to pay the estimated expenses of the State government, the interest of the State debt, and such deficiency as may occur in the resources.

2

STATUTORY PROVISIONS.

Act No. 164, Laws of 1881, as amended by Session Laws of 1883–85–87·89–93–95.

CHAPTER I.

THE SUPERINTENDENT OF PUBLIC INSTRUCTION.

Powers and duties of.

(§1.) SECTION 1. *The People of the State of Michigan enact,* That the Superintendent of Public Instruction shall have general supervision of public instruction and of all State institutions, other than the University, that are essentially educational in their character; and it shall be his duty among other things, to visit the University, the Agricultural College, the Institution for the Deaf and Dumb, the School for the Blind, the Industrial School for Boys, the Industrial School for Girls, and the Public School for Dependent and Neglected Children, and to meet with the governing boards of each of said institutions at last once *To make annual* in each year. He shall also prepare annually and trans-*report.* mit to the Governor, to be by him transmitted to the Legislature at each biennial session thereof, a report containing:

Contents of.

First, A statement of the condition of the University and of each of the several State educational institutions, all incorporated institutions of learning, and the primary, graded, and high schools;

Second, Estimates and amounts of expenditures of all educational funds;

Third, Plans for the management of all educational funds, and for the better organization of the educational system, if in his opinion the same be required;

Fourth, The annual reports and accompanying documents, so far as he shall deem the same of sufficient public interest, of all State institutions of educational character;

Fifth, Abstracts of the annual reports of the school inspectors of the several townships and cities of the State.

Sixth, All such other matter relating to his office and the subject of education generally, as he shall deem expedient to communicate.

Deputy Superintendent.

(§2.) SEC. 2. He may appoint a deputy superintendent of public instruction and revoke such appointment in his discretion, and such deputy shall take the constitutional oath of office which, with his appointment, shall be filed *Duties of.* with the Secretary of State. Said deputy may execute the duties of the office in case of a vacancy or the absence of the Superintendent.

(§3.) SEC. 3. The Superintendent of Public Instruction shall compile and cause to be printed all general laws relating to schools, together with all necessary forms, regulations, and instructions for conducting all proceedings under said laws, or relative to the organization and government of the schools, including rules and regulations for the management of township and district libraries, and shall transmit the same to the several officers entrusted with the care and management of said schools. School laws to be compiled and published with forms, etc.

(§4.) SEC. 4. He shall semi-annually, on receiving notice from the Auditor General of the amounts thereof, and between the first and tenth days of May and November, apportion the primary school interest fund among the several townships and cities of the State, in proportion to the number of children in each between the ages of five and twenty years, as the same shall appear by the reports of the several boards of school inspectors made to him for the school year closing prior to the May apportionment, and shall prepare a statement of the amount in the aggregate payable to each county, and shall deliver the same to the Auditor General, who shall thereupon draw his warrant upon the State Treasurer in favor of the treasurer of each county for the amount payable to each county. He shall also send written notices to the clerks of the several counties of the amount in the aggregate to be disbursed in their respective counties, and the amount payable to the townships and cities therein respectively. Apportionment of primary school fund, etc. See App. A, 154. Notice to county clerks of amounts disbursed.

(§5.) SEC. 5. Whenever the returns from any county, township, city, or district, upon which a statement of the amount to be disbursed or paid to any such county, township, city, or district shall be so far defective as to render it impracticable to ascertain the share of primary school interest fund which ought to be disbursed or paid to such county, township, city, or district, he shall ascertain by the best evidence in his power the facts upon which the ratio of such apportionment shall depend, and shall make the apportionment accordingly. Proceedings in case of defective returns.

(§6.) SEC. 6. Whenever any county, township, city, or district, through failure or error in making the proper report, shall fail to receive its share of the primary school interest fund, the Superintendent of Public Instruction, upon satisfactory proof that said county, township, city, or district was justly entitled to the same, shall apportion such deficiency in his next apportionment; and whenever it shall appear to the satisfaction of said Superintendent that any district has had three months' school, but failed to have the full time of school required by law, through no fault or negligence of the district or its officers, he may include such district in his apportionment of the primary school interest fund in his discretion. When deficiency may be apportioned the next year.

(§7.) SEC. 7. The Superintendent of Public Instruction shall perform such other duties as are or shall be required of him by law, and at the expiration of his term of office deliver to his successor all property, books, documents, Other duties of Superintendent.

maps, records, reports, and all other papers belonging to
his office or which may have been received by him for
the use of his office.

CHAPTER II.

FORMATION, ALTERATION, MEETINGS, AND POWERS OF DISTRICTS.

Inspectors to form districts.

(§8.) SECTION 1. The township board of school inspectors shall divide the township into such number of school
district as may from time to time be necessary, which districts they shall number; and they may regulate and alter
May alter boundaries of.
See App. A, ¶ 48.
the boundaries of the same as circumstances shall render
proper, subject to the provisions hereinafter made: but no
district shall contain more than nine sections of land, and
each district shall be composed of contiguous territory
and be in as compact a form as may be.

Township clerk to deliver notice of formation to inhabitant.
See App. B, forms 1, 2, 3.
(§9.) SEC. 2. Whenever the board of school inspectors
of any township shall form a school district therein, it
shall be the duty of the clerk of such board to deliver
to a taxable inhabitant of such district a notice in writing of the formation of such district, describing its boundaries, and specifying the time and place of the first meeting, which notice, with the fact of such delivery, shall be
Inhabitant to serve notice of first meeting.
See § 139.
entered upon record by the clerk. The said notice shall
also direct such inhabitant to notify every qualified voter
of such district, either personally or by leaving a written
notice at his place of residence, of the time and place of
said meeting, at least five days before the time appointed
therefor; and it shall be the duty of such inhabitant to
notify the qualified voters of said district accordingly, and
Return of notice.
said inhabitant, when he shall have notified the qualified
voters as required by such notice, shall endorse thereon
a return showing such notification with the date or dates
Notice and return to be recorded.
thereof, and deliver such notice and return to the chairman of the meeting, to be by him delivered to the
director chosen at such meeting, and by said director
recorded at length as a part of the records of such district.

Proceedings in case of failure to organize district.
(§10.) SEC. 3. In case the inhabitants of any district
shall fail to organize the same in pursuance of such
notice as aforesaid, the said clerk shall give a new notice
in the manner hereinbefore provided, and the same proceedings shall be had thereon as if no previous notice had
been delivered.

Formation of fractional districts.
(§11.) SEC. 4. Whenever it shall be necessary or con-
venient to form a district from two or more adjoining townships, the inspectors, or a majority of them, of each of
such adjoining townships, may form such district, to be
designated as a fractional district, and direct which township clerk shall make and deliver the notice of the formation of the same to a taxable inhabitant thereof, and may
regulate and alter such district as circumstances may ren-

der necessary in the same manner that other districts are altered. The annual reports of the director of such district shall be made to the inspectors of the township in which the schoolhouse may be situated, and the inspectors of such township shall number said district. To whom director of such district shall report.

(§12.) SEC. 5. Every such school district shall be deemed duly organized when any two of the officers elected at the first meeting shall have filed their acceptances in writing with the director, and the same shall have been recorded in the minutes of such first meeting. Every school district shall, in all cases, be presumed to have been legally organized, when it shall have exercised the franchises and privileges of a district for the term of two years; and such school district and its officers shall be entitled to all the rights, privileges, and immunities, and be subject to all the duties and liabilities conferred upon school districts by law. When district deemed organized. Presumption of legal organization. See App. A, ¶¶ 25, 29, 39, 47.

(§13.) SEC. 6. The record of the first meeting made by the director shall be *prima facie* evidence of the facts therein set forth, and of the legality of all proceedings in the organization of the district prior to the first district meeting; but nothing in this section contained shall be so construed as to impair the effect of the record kept by the school inspectors, as evidence. Director's record of first meeting to be evidence.

CORPORATE POWERS OF DISTRICTS.

(§14.) SEC. 7. Every school district organized in pursuance of this chapter, or which has been organized and continued under any previous law of the State or territory of Michigan, shall be a body corporate and shall possess the usual powers of a corporation for public purposes, by the name and style of "School District Number ——— (such number as shall be designated in the formation thereof by the inspectors), of ———" (the name of the township or townships in which the district is situated), and in that name shall be capable of suing and being sued, of contracting and being contracted with, and of holding such real and personal estate as is authorized to be purchased by the provisions of law, and of selling the same. School districts to be bodies corporate. Name and style. Powers of.

ALTERATION OF DISTRICTS.

(§15.) SEC. 8. Whenever the board of school inspectors shall contemplate an alteration of the boundaries of a district, the township clerk (and for meetings of boards to act in relation to fractional districts, clerks of the several townships interested) shall give at least ten days' notice of the time and place of the meeting of the inspectors and the alterations proposed, by posting such notice in three public places in the township or townships, one of which notices shall be in each of the districts that may Meetings of inspectors to alter districts. Notice of. See App. B, form 16.

be affected by such alteration. Whenever the board of school inspectors of more than one township meet, they shall elect one of their number chairman and another clerk thereof.

(§16.) SEC. 9. The inspectors may, in their discretion, detach the property of any person or persons from one district and attach it to another, except that no land
which has been taxed for building a schoolhouse shall be set off into another school district for the period of three years thereafter, except by the consent of the owner
thereof; and no district shall be divided into two or more districts without the consent of a majority of the resident taxpayers of said district, and no two or more districts be consolidated without the consent of a majority of the resident taxpayers of each district.

(§17.) SEC. 10. The inspectors may attach to a school district any person residing in a township and not in any organized district, at his request; and for all district purposes except raising a tax for building a schoolhouse, such person shall be considered as residing in such district, but when set off to a new district, no sum shall be raised for such person as his proportion to the district property.

(§18.) SEC. 11. In all cases where an alteration of the boundaries of a school district shall be made, the township clerk shall, within ten days, deliver to the director of each
district affected by the alteration, a notice in writing setting forth the action of the inspectors and defining the alterations that have been made.

DIVISION OF PROPERTY.

(§19.) SEC. 12. When a new district is formed in whole or in part, from one or more districts possessed of a school house or entitled to other property, the inspectors, at the
time of forming such new district or as soon thereafter as may be, shall ascertain and determine the amount justly due to such new district from any district out of which it may have been in whole or in part formed, as the proportion of such new district, of the value of the school house and other property belonging to the former district,
at the time of such division; and whenever by the division of any district, the schoolhouse or site thereof shall no longer be conveniently located for school purposes and shall
not be desired for use by the new district in which it may be situated, the school inspectors of the township in which
such schoolhouse and site shall be located, may advertise and sell the same, and apportion the proceeds of such sale and also any moneys belonging to the district thus

(§19.) Upon investigation we are of the opinion that the school inspectors of the township have full and absolute control over the advertisement, sale, and apportionment of the proceeds among the several districts, erected in whole or in part therefrom.—*Van Riper, Attorney General, July 24, 1882.*

divided, among the several districts erected in whole or in part from the divided district.

(§20.) SEC. 13. Such proportion shall be ascertained and *How proportion to be ascertained.* determined according to the value of the taxable property of the respective parts of such former district at the time of the division, by the best evidence in the power of the inspectors; and such amount of any debt due from the former district which would have been a charge upon the new, had it remained in the former district, shall be deducted from such proportion: *Provided,* That no real *Proviso.* estate thus set off, and which shall not have been taxed for the purchase or building of such schoolhouse, shall be entitled to any portion thereof, nor be taken into account in such division of district property.

DISTRICT MEETINGS.

(§21.) SEC. 14. The annual meeting of each school dis- *Annual meeting.* trict shall be held on the first Monday of September in each year, and the school year shall commence on that day: *Provided,* That any school district that shall so determine *School year.* at an annual meeting, or at a special meeting duly called for that purpose, may hold its annual meeting on the second Monday of July in each year, or in the same *Date of annual meeting may* manner may thereafter change the time of its annual *be changed.* meeting to the first Monday in September in each year; and the trustees and officers of the district shall date their terms of office from the date so chosen and until their successors are elected and qualified: *Provided, fur-* *Proviso.* *ther,* That such action in either case shall not change the time of the commencement of the school year or the taking of the annual school census.

(§22.) SEC. 15. Special meetings may be called by the *Special meet-* district board; and it shall be the duty of said board, or *ings.* any of them, to call such meetings on the written request of not less than five legal voters of the district, by giv- *See App. B, form 8.* ing the notice required in the next succeeding section; but no special meeting shall be called, unless the business *When may not be called.* to be transacted may lawfully come before such meeting, and no business shall be transacted at a special meeting *Business of to be stated in* unless the same be stated in the notice of said meeting. *notice.*

(§23.) SEC. 16. All notices of annual or special district *Notice of meetings.* meetings, after the first meeting has been held as aforesaid, shall specify the day and hour and place of meet- *See App. B, forms 7, 9.* ing, and shall be given at least six days previous to such meeting, by posting up copies thereof in three of the most public places in the district, one copy of which for each meeting shall be posted at the outer door of the district schoolhouse, if there be one; and in case of any special meeting called for the purpose of establishing or changing the site of a schoolhouse, such notice shall be given at least ten days previous thereto: *Provided,* That when any *Duty of district* of the district board shall receive a request to call a special *officer to give notice.*

meeting, as provided in the preceding section, he shall forthwith give notice, as above provided, of said meeting, which shall be called in not, less than six nor more than twelve days from the time the said officer shall receive the notice aforesaid. No annual meeting shall be deemed illegal for want of due notice, unless it shall appear that the omission to give such notice was wilful and fraudulent.

(§24.) Sec. 17. Every citizen* of the age of twenty-one years, who has property assessed for school taxes in any school district and who has resided therein three months next preceding any school meeting held in said district, or who has resided three months next preceding such meeting on any territory belonging to such district at the time of holding said meeting, shall be a qualified voter in said meeting upon all questions, and all other citizens* who are twenty-one years of age and are the parents or legal guardians of any children included in the school census of the district, and who have for three months as aforesaid, been residents of said district or upon any territory belonging thereto at the time of holding any school meeting, shall be entitled to vote on all questions arising in said district which do not directly involve the raising of money by tax.

(§25.) Sec. 18. If any person offering to vote at a school district meeting shall be challenged as unqualified, by any legal voter in such district, the chairman presiding at such meeting shall declare to the person challenged, the qualifications of a voter; and if such person shall state that he is qualified and the challenge shall not be withdrawn, the chairman shall tender to him an oath in substance as follows: "You do swear (or affirm) that you are a citizen[b] of the United States, that you have been for the last three months an actual resident of this school district or residing upon territory now attached to this school district, and that you pay a school district tax therein;" and every person taking this oath shall be permitted to vote upon all questions proposed at such meetings. Or he may take the following oath, to wit: "You do swear (or affirm) that you are a citizen[b] of the United States, that you have been for the last three months an actual resident of this school district or residing upon territory now attached to this school district, and that you are the parent or legal guardian of one or more childen now included in the school census of the district;" and he may vote upon all questions which do not directly involve the raising of money by tax. If any person so challenged shall refuse to take such oath. his vote shall be rejected; and any person who shall wilfully take a false oath or make a false affirmation, under the

* Amended by Act No. 15, Public Acts of 1895.
b Amended by Act No. 258, Public Acts of 1895.

provisions of this section, shall be deemed guilty of perjury. When any question is taken in any other way than by ballot, a challenge immediately after the vote has been taken shall be deemed to be made when offering the vote and treated in the same manner.

(§26.) SEC. 19. If at any district meeting any person Disorderly persons at district shall conduct himself in a disorderly manner and, after meetings to be taken into notice from the moderator or person presiding, shall persist therein, the moderator or person presiding may order custody. him to withdraw from the meeting, and on his refusal, may order any constable, or other person or persons, to take him into custody until the meeting shall be adjourned; and any person who shall refuse to withdraw from such Penalty for disturbing meeting on being so ordered as herein provided, and also ing. any person who shall wilfully disturb such meeting by rude and indecent behavior, or by profane or indecent discourse, or in any other way make such disturbance, shall, on conviction thereof, be punished by a fine not less than two nor more than fifty dollars, or by imprisonment in the county jail not exceeding thirty days; and any justice of the peace, recorder, or police justice of the Who shall have jurisdiction township, ward, or city where such offense shall be committed, shall have jurisdiction to, try and determine the same.

(§27.) SEC. 20. The qualified voters in any school dis-Powers of voters at district trict when lawfully assembled at the first and at each meetings. annual meeting, or at any adjournment thereof, or at any special meeting lawfully called, except as hereinafter provided, shall have power:

First, At the first meeting and at any meeting after the To appoint temporary officers. organization of the district, in the absence of the moderator, to appoint a chairman for the time being, and in the absence of the director to appoint some person to act in his stead, who shall keep a minute of the proceedings of such meeting and certify the same to the director, to be by him entered in the records of the district;

Second, To adjourn from time to time as occasion may May adjourn. require;

Third, To elect district officers as hereinafter provided; To elect officers. See §§ 28, 107.

Fourth, To designate, as hereinafter provided, a site or To designate sites for schoolhouses, such number of sites as may be desired for schoolhouses, houses. and to change the same when necessary; See § 89.

Fifth, To direct the purchasing or leasing of a site or To direct purchase, etc., of site, and building sites, lawfully determined upon; the building, hiring, or purchasing of a schoolhouse or houses, or the enlarging ing school-houses. of a site or sites previously established;

Sixth, To vote such tax as the meeting shall deem To vote tax for building, etc. sufficient, to purchase or lease a site or sites, or to build,

(§27, ¶ eight.) All sales thus made shall be in the corporate name of the school district, as provided in Section 7, Chapter 2, of said Act 164, while the deed or deeds of the conveyance of lands sold as above provided shall be executed by the district board in their official capacity, but in the name of such district.—*Van Riper, Atty. Gen., July 24, 1882.*

3

<table>
</table>

Limit of tax.

See § 78.

hire, or purchase a schoolhouse or houses: but the amount of taxes to be raised in any district for the purpose of purchasing or building a schoolhouse or houses in the same year that any bonded indebtedness is incurred, shall not exceed in districts containing less than ten children between the ages of five and twenty years, two hundred fifty dollars; in districts having between ten and thirty children of like age, it shall not exceed five hundred dollars; and in districts having between thirty and fifty children of like age, it shall not exceed one thousand dollars.

When land not taxable.

No legal subdivisions [subdivision] of land shall be taxed for building a schoolhouse, unless some portion thereof shall be within two and one-half miles of said schoolhouse site;

To vote tax for certain purposes.
See App. A, ¶¶ 97, 101.

Seventh, To impose such tax as shall be necessary to keep their schoolhouse or houses in repair, and to provide the necessary appendages and school apparatus, and in districts having district libraries, for the support of the same, and to pay and discharge any debts or liabilities of the district lawfully incurred, and also to pay for the services of any district officer. The tax herein authorized to be voted shall not exceed one-half the amount which the district is authorized to raise for building schoolhouses;

Limit of tax.

To direct sale of certain property.

Eighth, To authorize and direct the sale of any schoolhouse, site, building, or other property belonging to the district, when the same shall no longer be needed for the use of the district;

Direct in regard to suits.

Ninth, To give such directions and make such provisions as they shall deem necessary in relation to the prosecution or defense of any suit or proceeding in which the district may be a party, or interested;

May appoint building committee.

Tenth, To appoint, as in their discretion it may be necessary, a building committee to perform such duties in supervising the work of building a schoolhouse, as they by vote may direct;

At annual meeting to determine limit of school.

Eleventh, *At the first and the annual meeting only, to determine the length of time a school shall be taught in their district during the ensuing year, which shall not be less than nine months in districts having eight hundred children over five and under twenty years of age, and not

Forfeiture of public moneys.

less than five months in all other districts, on pain of forfeiture of their share of the primary school interest fund; but in case such matters shall not be determined at the first or annual meeting, the district board shall determine

When district board to determine length of school.

the same; and in case the district fails to vote for at least the minimum length required herein, the district board shall make provisions for said minimum length of school;

May appropriate surplus mill tax to certain purposes.

Twelfth, To appropriate any surplus moneys arising from the one-mill tax, after having maintained a school in the district at least eight months in the school year, for the

* Amended by Act No. 15, Public Acts of 1895.

purpose of purchasing and enlarging school sites, or for
building or repairing schoolhouses, or for purchasing books
for library, globes, maps, and other school apparatus, or for
any incidental expenses of the school.

CHAPTER III.

DISTRICT BOARD AND OFFICERS.

(§28.) SECTION 1. At the first meeting in each school *Election of district officers.*
district there shall be elected by ballot a moderator for *See App. A,*
the term of three years, a director for two years, and an *¶¶ 151, 152.*
assessor for one year; and on the expiration of their *See §§ 140, 147.*
respective terms of office, and regularly thereafter at the *See App. A, ¶ 49.*
annual meetings, their several successors shall be elected
in like manner for a term of three years each. The time *Term of office.*
intervening between the first meeting in any school district and the first annual meeting thereafter shall be
reckoned as one year.

(§29.) SEC. 2. A school district office shall become *When district offices shall become vacant.*
vacant upon the occurrence of any of the following events:
First, The death of the incumbent;
Second, His resignation;
Third, His removal from office;
Fourth, His removal from the district;
Fifth, His conviction of any infamous crime;
Sixth, His election or appointment being declared void
by a competent tribunal;
Seventh, His neglect to file his acceptance of office, or
to give or renew any official bond, according to law.

(§30.) SEC. 3. In case any one of the district offices *Vacancies in office, how filled.*
becomes vacant, the two remaining officers shall imme-
diately fill such vacancy; or in case two of the offices
become vacant, the remaining officer shall immediately call
a special meeting of the district to fill such vacancies;
in case any vacancy is not filled as herein provided, within *See App. B, forms 14, 15.*
twenty days after it shall have occurred, or in case all
the offices in a district shall become vacant, the board of
school inspectors of the township to which the annual
reports of such district are made shall fill such vacancies.
Any person elected or appointed to fill a vacancy in a *Term of office of appointed officer.*
district office shall hold such office until the next suc-
ceeding annual meeting, at which time the voters of the
district shall fill such office for the unexpired portion of
the term.

(§28.) School district officers cannot be elected by a bare plurality vote. In electing
officers the school district acts in its corporate capacity, and no corporate action can be
had without the concurrence of the majority.—*Kirchner, Atty. Gen., July 19, 1877.*

(§29.) The temporary absence of the assessor does not create a vacancy in the office.
If his family continues to reside in the district and he has not actually removed, he
retains his residence and with it his office. A removal is necessary; and a temporary
absence, his family remaining, is not a removal and there is no vacancy.—*Van Riper
Atty. Gen., Feb. 3, 1932.*

Who are eligible to hold office. (§31.) Sec. 4. Any qualified voter in a school district who has property liable to assessment for school taxes shall be eligible to election or appointment to office in such school district, unless such person be an alien.

Acceptances of offices to be filed. (§32.) Sec. 5. Within ten days after their election or appointment, the several officers of each school district shall file with the director written acceptances of the

See App. B, form 5. offices to which they have been respectively elected or appointed, and such acceptances shall be entered in the records of the district by said director.

District board, when meetings of may be called. (§33.) Sec. 6. The moderator, director, and assessor shall constitute the district board. Meetings of the board may be called by any member thereof by serving on the other members a written notice of the time and place of such meeting at least twenty-four hours before such meeting is

Necessity of meeting to valid action by board. to take place; and no act authorized to be done by the district board shall be valid, unless voted at a meeting of

Quorum of board. the board. A majority of the members of the board at a meeting thereof shall be necessary for the transaction of business.

Board to purchase record books, etc. (§34.) Sec. 7. The said district board shall purchase a record book, and such other books, blanks, and stationery as may be necessary to keep a record of the proceedings

See App. A, ¶ 103. of the district meetings and of meetings of the board, the accounts of the assessor, and for doing the business of the district in an orderly manner.

Board to purchase site and build schoolhouse. (§35.) Sec. 8. The district board shall purchase or lease, in the corporate name of the district, such sites for schoolhouses as shall have been lawfully designated, and shall

See App. A, ¶¶ 114, 124. build, hire, or purchase such schoolhouses as may be necessary out of the fund provided for that purpose, and

Necessity of title or lease to site before building schoolhouse. make sale of any site or other property of the district when lawfully directed by the qualified voters; but no district in any case shall build a stone or brick schoolhouse upon any site without having first obtained a title in fee to the same or a lease for ninety-nine years; nor shall

See App. B, forms 23, 24, 25. any district build a frame schoolhouse on any site for which they have not a title in fee or a lease for fifty years, without securing the privilege of removing the said schoolhouse, when lawfully directed so to do by the qualified voters of the district at any annual or special meeting when lawfully convened.

Board to estimate tax for support of schools. (§36.) Sec. 9. It shall be the duty of the district board to estimate the amount necessary to be raised in addition

(§33.) The district board should act together. It is not necessary for valid official action that all the members should be consulted, but opportunity must be given to all the members to express their opinion and to vote upon the questions submitted to them. —*Kirchner, Atty. Gen., Dec. 4, 1877.*

(§33.) Whenever a power is vested in a board for a public purpose, it requires a quorum to act and a majority of that quorum to determine a matter before it.—*Kirchner, Atty. Gen., Apr. 7, 1879.*

(§35.) The record of a lease for a term of years is not essential to its validity, though leases for a longer term than three years should be recorded, in order to render them effectual against subsequent purchasers in good faith and for a valuable consideration. The non-payment of rent does not *ipso facto* terminate the lease.—*Kirchner, Atty. Gen., Sept. 26, 1877.*

to other school funds, for the entire support of such schools, including teachers' wages, fuel, and other incidental expenses, and for deficiencies of the previous year for such purposes. But in districts having less than thirty scholars, such esti- *Limit of tax in certain cases.* mate, including the district's share of the primary school interest fund and one-mill tax, shall not exceed the sum of fifty dollars a month for the period during which school is held in such district; and when such amount has been estimated and voted by the district board, it shall be reported for assessment and collection, the same as other district taxes. When a tax has been estimated *When board may borrow* and voted by the district board under the provisions of *money.* this section, and is needed before it can be collected, the district board may borrow to an amount not exceeding the amount of said tax.

(§37.) SEC. 10. The district board shall, between the *Board to report district taxes* first and third Mondays in September in each year, make *to township clerk.* out and deliver to the township clerk of each township in which any part of the district is situated, a report in *See App. B, form 12.* writing under their hands of all taxes voted by the district during the preceding year and of all taxes which said board is authorized to impose, to be levied on the taxable property of the district.

(§38.) SEC. 11. The district board shall apply and pay *Board to apply moneys accord-* over all school moneys belonging to the district, in accord- *ing to law.* ance with the provisions of law regulating the same; and no money raised by district tax shall be used for any other purpose than that for which it was raised, without a consenting vote of two-thirds of the tax paying voters of the district; and no moneys received from the primary school interest fund, nor from the one-mill tax, except as provided by law, shall be appropriated to any other use than the payment of teachers' wages, and no part thereof shall be paid to any teacher who shall not have received a certificate of qualification from proper legal authority before the commencement of his school. No school dis- *Sectarian schools barred* trict shall apply any of the moneys received by it from *from public* the primary school interest fund or from any and all *moneys.* other sources, for the support and maintenance of any school of a sectarian character, whether the same be under the control of any religious society or made sectarian by the school district board.

(§39.) SEC. 12. Said board shall present to the district, *Board to make annual report.* at each annual meeting, a report in writing, containing an accurate statement of all moneys of the district received by them, or any of them, during the preceding year, and of the disbursements made by them, with the items of such receipts and disbursements. Such report shall also *Contents of.* contain a statement of all taxes assessed upon the taxable property of the district during the preceding year, the pur-

(§38.) I am inclined to think that no money raised by district taxes can be used for any other purpose than that for which it was raised, unless by vote of two-thirds of the tax paying voters of the district. I think this section must be strictly and literally observed —*Kirchner, Atty. Gen., Sept. 26, 1877.*

poses for which such taxes were assessed, and the amount assessed for each particular purpose; and said report shall be entered by the director in the records of the district.

Board to hire teachers.
See App. B, forms 26, 27.
Contracts.

(§40.) SEC. 13. The district board shall hire and contract with such duly qualified teachers as may be required; and all contracts shall be in writing and signed by a majority of the board on behalf of the district. Said contracts shall specify the wages agreed upon and shall require the teacher to keep a correct list of the pupils, and the age of each attending the school, and the number of days each pupil is present, and to furnish the director with a correct copy of the same at the close of the school. Said contract shall be filed with the director, and a duplicate copy of the contract shall be furnished to the teacher. No contract with any person not holding a legal certificate of qualification then authorizing such person to teach shall be valid; and all such contracts shall terminate, if the certificate shall expire by limitation and shall not immediately be renewed, or if it shall be suspended or revoked by proper legal authority. A school month within the meaning of the school laws shall consist of four weeks of five days in each week, unless otherwise specified in the teacher's contract.

School register to be kept.
See § 147.
Contracts to be filed.
Teacher must have legal certificate.
See App. A, ¶¶ 79, 88, 90, 91, 92, 93, 94.
School month defined.

Care and use of schoolhouse.

(§41.) SEC. 14. The district board shall have the care and custody of the schoolhouse and other property of the district, except so far as the same shall by vote of the district be specially confided to the custody of the director, including all books purchased for the use of indigent pupils, and shall open the schoolhouse for public meetings, unless by a vote at a district meeting it shall be determined otherwise: *Provided*, That said board may exclude such public meetings during the five school days of each week of any and all school terms or such parts thereof as in their discretion they may deem for the best interests of the schools.

Board may exclude public meetings at certain times.

Board to specify studies and prescribe text-books.

(§42.) SEC. 15. The district board shall specify the studies to be pursued in the schools of the district [districts] and, in addition to the branches in which instruction is now required by law to be given in the public schools of the State, instruction shall be given in physiology and hygiene with a special reference to the nature of alcohol and narcotics and their effects upon the human system. Such instruction shall be given by the aid of text-books in the case of pupils who are able to read and as thoroughly as in other studies pursued in the same school. The text-books to be used for such instruction shall give at least one-fourth of their space to the consideration of the nature and effects of alcoholic drinks and narcotics, and the books used in the highest grade of graded schools shall contain at least twenty pages of matter relating to this subject. Text-books used in giving the foregoing instruction shall first be approved by the State Board of Education. Each school board making a

Instruction in physiology and hygiene, required.

Text-books in physiology, etc., to be approved by State board of education.

selection of text-books under the provisions of this act shall make a record thereof in their proceedings; and text-books once adopted under the provisions of this act shall not be changed within five years, except by a consent of a majority of the qualified voters of the district present at an annual meeting or at a special meeting called for that purpose. The district board shall require each teacher in the public schools of such district, before placing the school register in the hands of the directors [director] as provided in section thirteen of this act, to certify therein whether or not instruction has been given in the school or grade presided over by such teacher as required by this act; and it shall be the duty of the director of the district to file with the township clerk a certified copy of such certificate. Any school board neglecting or refusing to comply with any of the provisions of this act shall be subject to fine or forfeiture, the same as for neglect of any other duty pertaining to their office. This act shall apply to all schools in the State, including schools in cities or villages, whether incorporated under special charter or under the general laws.

(§43.) SEC. 16. The district board may purchase at the expense of the district such text-books as may be necessary for the use of children, when parents are not able to furnish the same; and they shall include the amount of such purchase in the report to the township clerk or clerks, to be levied in like manner as other district taxes. *Purchase of books for poor children.*

(§44.) SEC. 17. The district board shall have the general care of the school, and shall make and enforce suitable rules and regulations for its government and management and for the preservation of the property of the district. Said board may authorize or order the suspension or expulsion from the school, whenever in its judgment the interests of the school demand it, of any pupil guilty of gross misdemeanor or persistent disobedience. Any person who shall disturb any school by rude and indecent behavior, or by profane or indecent discourse, or in any other way make such disturbance, shall on conviction thereof be punished by a fine not less than two nor more than fifty dollars or by imprisonment in the county jail not exceeding thirty days. *Board to establish rules for school. See App. A, ¶ 64. May suspend or expel disorderly pupils. Penalty for disturbing school.*

(§45.) SEC. 18. All persons residents of any school district and five years of age shall have an equal right to attend any school therein, and no separate school or *Who can attend school.*

(§44.) It is not competent for the district board to assume the expense incurred in the legal defense of a teacher prosecuted for an assault alleged to have been made in the punishment of a pupil.—*Kirchner, Attorney General, Dec. 4, 1877.*

(§45.) The domicile of any person is the place which he has chosen for his permanent residence. Sometimes the law makes a distinction between "residence" and "domicile." Residence, contra distinguished from domicile, is the locality in which a person may reside for the time being. But in the case under consideration the term residence is used in the sense of domicile. I have no doubt that a person who makes Flint his or her home for no other purpose than to enjoy school privileges and with the intention of removing to his or her former home after the closing of the school, is "not actually a resident of said district." A minor having parents living, partakes of the domicile of his or her parents.—*Kirchner, Attorney General, Jan. 25, 1879.*

No separate school on account of race, etc.

See App. A, ¶ 113.

Grading not prevented.

Non-resident pupils' tuition.

department shall be kept for any persons on account of race or color: *Provided,* That this shall not be construed to prevent the grading of schools according to the intellectual progress of the pupil, to be taught in separate places as may be deemed expedient.

(§46.)* SEC. 19. The district board may admit to the district school non-resident pupils, and may determine the rates of tuition of such pupils and collect the same, which tuition shall not be greater than fifteen per cent more than the average cost per capita for the number of pupils of school age in the district. Children who are being cared for at county expense shall be admitted to the school in the district whose schoolhouse is nearest the county house, on the same terms that other non-resident pupils are admitted. When non-resident pupils (their parents or guardians) pay a school tax in said district, such pupils shall be admitted to the schools of the district, and the amount of such school tax shall be credited on their tuition, a sum not to exceed the amount of such tuition, and they shall only be required to pay tuition for the difference therein.

Proviso.

Moderator.

(§47.) SEC. 20. It shall be the duty of the moderator of each school district:

To preside.

First, To preside, when present, at all meetings of the district and of the board;

To countersign warrants and orders.

Second, To countersign all orders legally drawn by the director upon the assessor for moneys to be disbursed by the district, and all warrants of the director upon the township treasurer for moneys raised for district purposes or apportioned to the district by the township clerk;

See App. A, ¶¶ 55, 57.

To bring suit on assessor's bond.

Third, To cause an action to be prosecuted in the name of the district on the assessor's bond, in case of any breach of any condition thereof;

Other duties.

Fourth, To perform such other duties as are or shall be by law required of the moderator.

DIRECTOR.

Director.

(§48.) SEC. 21. It shall be the duty of the director of each school district:

To be clerk.

First, To act as clerk, when present, at all meetings of the district and of the board;

To keep and record minutes.

Second, To record the proceedings of all district meetings, and the minutes of all meetings, orders, resolutions, and other proceedings of the board, in proper record books;

To give notices of meetings.

Third, To give the prescribed notice of the annual district meeting, and of all such special meetings as he shall be required to give notice of in accordance with the provisions of law;

See App. B, forms 7, 9.

---

* Amended by Act No. 131, Public Acts of 1895.

(§47.) The moderator should examine every order before countersigning it, and if it is drawn for an improper purpose and with intent to defraud the district or to divert the fund from its proper channel, he should refuse to countersign such order; and the courts will sustain him in such action.—*Van Riper, Attorney General, Feb. 8, 1882.*

Fourth, To draw and sign warrants upon the township treasurer for all moneys raised for district purposes or apportioned to the district by the township clerk, payable to the assessor of the district, and orders upon the assessor for all moneys to be disbursed by the district, and present them to the moderator, to be countersinged by that officer. Each order shall specify the object for which, and the fund upon which, it is drawn; <small>To draw and sign warrants and orders. See App. A. ¶¶ 50, 66.</small>

<small>See App. B, forms 10, 11.</small>

Fifth, To draw and sign all contracts with teachers, when directed by the district board, and present them to the other members of the board for further signature; <small>To draw and sign contracts. See App. B, form 26.</small>

Sixth, To provide the necessary appendages for the schoolhouse, and keep the same in good condition and repair during the time school shall be taught therein. Necessary appendages within the meaning of law shall consist of the following articles, to wit: a set of wall maps (the grand divisions, the United States, and Michigan) not exceeding twelve dollars in price; a globe not exceeding eight dollars; a dictionary not exceeding ten dollars; a reading chart not exceeding five dollars, and a case for library books not exceeding ten dollars; also looking-glass, comb, towel, water-pail, cup, ash-pail, poker, stove-shovel, broom, dust-pan, duster, wash-basin and soap. <small>To provide appendages and keep schoolhouse in repair.</small>

<small>Proviso. See App. A, ¶¶ 99, 101.</small>

Seventh, To keep an accurate account of all expenses incurred by him as director, and such account shall be audited by the moderator and assessor, and on their written order shall be paid out of any money provided for the purpose; <small>To keep account.</small>

Eighth, To present at each annual meeting an estimate of the expenses necessary to be incurred during the ensuing year by the director as provided by law, and for payment of the services of any district officer; <small>To present estimates of expenses to annual meeting.</small>

Ninth, To preserve and file copies of all reports made to the school inspectors, and safely preserve and keep all books, papers, and other documents belonging to the office of director, or to the district when not otherwise provided for, and to deliver the same to his successor in office; <small>To preserve records and other documents.</small>

Tenth, To perform such other duties as are or shall be required of the director by law or the district board. <small>Other duties.</small>

(§49.) SEC. 22. It shall be the duty of the director or such other person as the district board may appoint, within ten days next previous to the first Monday in September in each year, to take the census of the district and make a list in writing of the names and ages <small>To take school census.</small>

<small>List to be sworn to,</small>

---

* As amended by Act No. 258, Public Acts of 1895.

(§48, paragraph 6.) I think the director has power to provide new patent seats, if in his judgment such acquisition is "necessary." It is a general principle of law that whenever a power may be exercised by any person in certain emergencies, in the absence of any provision to the contrary, the person who is to execute the power must decide whether the emergency is sufficient for him to act. The director must decide what is necessary and he is responsible for any abuse of power. The word "necessary" as used in Sec. 48, must not be understood in its literal sense; *i. e.*, things that cannot be done without. In such a sense none of the conveniences and apparatus found in schools would be necessary. I take it that all such things are necessary which, in the judgment of the director, would promote the efficiency and welfare of the school, having due regard to all the circumstances of the case.—*Kirchner, Atty. Gen., July 31, 1877.*

4

•

of all the children between the ages of five and twenty years residing therein; and a copy of said list shall be verified by the oath or affirmation of the person taking such census, by affidavit appended thereto or endorsed thereon, setting forth that it is a correct list of the names of all the children between the ages aforesaid residing in the district, which affidavit may be made before the clerk of the township; and said list shall be returned with the annual report of the director to the township clerk. Children in almshouses, prisons, or asylums, not otherwise residents of the district and not attending the school, shall not be included in the said census; nor shall Indian children be so included, unless they attend the school or their parents are liable to pay taxes therein.

(§50.) SEC. 23. The director shall also, at the end of the school year and previous to the second Monday in September in each year, deliver to the township clerk, to be filed in his office, a report to the board of school inspectors of the township, showing:

First, The whole number of children belonging to the district between the ages of five and twenty years, according to the census taken as aforesaid;

Second, The number attending school during the year under five, and also the number over twenty years of age;

Third, The number of non-resident pupils of the district that have attended school during the year;

Fourth, The whole number that have attended school during the year;

Fifth, The length of time the school has been taught during the year by a qualified teacher, the name of each teacher, the length of time taught by each, and the wages paid to each;

Sixth, The average length of time scholars between five and twenty years of age, have attended school during the year;

Seventh, The amount of money received from the township treasurer apportioned to the district by the township clerk;

Eighth, The amount of money raised by the district, and the purposes for which it was raised;

Ninth, The kind of books used in the school;

Tenth, Such other facts and statistics in regard to the schools and the subject of education as the Superintendent of Public Instruction shall direct.

(§51.) SEC. 24. The director of each fractional district shall make his annual report to the clerk of the township in which the schoolhouse is situated, and shall also report to the clerk of each township in which the district is in part situated, the number of children between the ages of five and twenty years in that part of the district lying in such township.

ASSESSOR.

(§52.) Sec. 25. It shall be the duty of assessor of each chool district: *Assessor. See App. A, ¶¶ 50, 66.*

First, To execute to the district and file with the lirector within ten days after his election or appointment, . bond in double the amount of money to come into his iands as such assessor during his tèrm of office, as near as he same can be ascertained, with two sufficient sureties. o be approved by, the moderator and director, conditioned or the faithful application of all moneys that shall come nto his hands by virtue of his office, and to perform all .he duties of his said office as required by the provisions)f this act. Said bond shall be filed with the director ind, in case of any breach of the condition thereof, the noderator shall cause a suit to be commenced thereon in ;he name of the district; and any moneys collected thereon iball be paid into the township treasury, subject to the)rder of the district officers, and shall be applied to the jame purposes as the moneys lost should have been ipplied by the assessor; *To give bond. See App. B, form 6. Bond to be approved. Bond filed with director. When suit to be brought thereon*

Second, To pay all orders of the director, when lawfully lrawn and countersigned by the moderator, out of any moneys in his hands belonging to the fund upon which such orders may be drawn; *To pay proper orders.*

Third, To keep a book in which all the moneys received and disbursed shall be entered, the sources from which the same have been received, and the persons to whom and the objects for which the same have been paid; *To keep record of receipts and disbursements.*

Fourth, To present to the district board at the close of the school year a report in writing, containing a statement of all moneys received during the preceding year and of each item of disbursements made, and exhibit the voucher therefor; *To make annual report to district board.*

Fifth, To appear for and on behalf of the district in all suits brought by or against the same, when no other directions shall be given by the qualified voters in district meeting, except in suits in which he is interested adversely to *To appear for district in suits. See App. A, ¶¶ 108, 109.*

(§52.) Is a district assessor justifiable under the law in refusing to pay an order drawn for any purpose not authorized by law, although such order is duly signed by the director and countersigned by the moderator? Cases may arise in which the assessor is in duty bound not to pay such orders.—*Kirchner, Atty. Gen., May 22, 1890.*

(§52.) The sureties on a bond executed by the assessor of the school district are not responsible for acts or omissions occurring beyond the period for which the assessor was elected. In case of his reelection a new bond should be given.—*Kirchner, Atty. Gen., Dec. 4, 1877.*

(§52.) Mr. S. was elected to the office of assessor of a school district and gave the requisite bonds. Since his first election he has been re-elected but has never executed any additional bonds. He has never been requested so to do by the moderator and director. Laterally the director requested him to execute an official bond and S. replied that he could not do so just then, and thereupon and without any further proceedings the district treated the office of assessor as vacant and proceeded at once to an election to fill said supposed vacancy. I am entirely clear that Mr. S. has not forfeited his office and that he is not only justified, but it is his duty not to pass over any of the papers pertaining to the office or any of the school district's moneys; but Mr. S. should give bonds at once. Both the director and moderator were derelict in their duty in failing to require the bond of the assessor at the outset. After filing the bond Mr. S. should continue to administer the office of assessor.—*Kirchner, Atty. Gen., Sept. 15, 1879.*

the district; and in all such cases the moderator shall appear for such district, if no other direction be given as aforesaid;

To deliver to his successor books, papers, etc. *Sixth*, At the close of his term of office to settle with the district board, and deliver to his successor in office all books, vouchers, orders, documents, and papers belonging to the office of assessor, together with all district moneys remaining on hand;

Other duties. *Seventh*, To perform such other duties as are or shall be by law required of the assessor.

CHAPTER IV.

TOWNSHIP OFFICERS.

TOWNSHIP BOARD OF SCHOOL INSPECTORS.

Board of school inspectors. (§53.) SECTION 1. The school inspectors of each township, together with the township clerk, shall constitute the township board of school inspectors. Said board shall meet within twenty days after the first Monday in April in each year, and elect one of their number, other than the township clerk, chairman of said board, and the township clerk shall be the clerk thereof.

See §§ 142, 148.

Chairman of board to be treasurer. (§54.) SEC. 2. The chairman of said board shall be the treasurer thereof, and shall give bond to the township in *To give bond.* double the amount of moneys to come into his hands during his term of office, as near as the same can be ascertained, with two sufficient sureties, to be approved by the *See App. B, form 13.* township clerk, conditioned for the faithful appropriation of all moneys that may come into his hands by virtue of *Bond to be filed.* his office. Said bond shall be filed with the township clerk and, in case of the non-fulfilment thereof, said clerk *When suit to be brought thereon,* shall cause a suit to be commenced thereon, and the moneys collected in such suit shall be paid into the township treasury and shall be applied to the same purposes as the moneys lost should have been applied by said treasurer of the board of school inspectors.

Inspectors to make triplicate report. (§55.) SEC. 3. On the third Monday in September in each year, the inspectors shall make triplicate reports setting forth the whole number of districts in their townships, the amount of money raised and received for township and *Contents of.* district libraries, and such other items as shall from year to year be required by the Superintendent of Public Instruction, together with the several particulars set forth in the reports of the school directors for the preceding *Disposition of reports.* year; and the township clerk shall, within ten days thereafter, forward two copies of the same to the secretary [com-

---

(§53.) When the inspectors fail to elect a chairman within twenty days after the first Monday of April, I am of the opinion that the organization can be perfected after such date by the election of a chairman, and that failure to comply with the law referred to does not preclude a legal organization thereafter.—*Taggart, Atty. Gen., May 20, 1886.*

nissioner] of the county board of school examiners, and ile the other copy in his office.

(§56.) SEC. 4. It shall be the duty of the school inspectors, before making their annual report, as required by the preceding section, to examine the list of legally qualified teachers on file in the office of the township clerk; and if in any school district a school shall not have been taught for the time required by law during the preceding school year by a legally qualified teacher, no part of the public money shall be distributed to such district, although the report from such district shall set forth that a school has been so taught; and it shall be the duty of the board to certify to the facts in relation to any such district in their annual report. *Inspectors to examine list of qualified teachers.* *To report districts not employing such.*

(§57.) SEC. 5. It shall be the duty of the board of inspectors to render to the township board, on the Tuesday next preceding the annual township meeting, a full and true account of all moneys received and disbursed by them as such inspectors during the year, which account shall be settled by said township board and such disbursements allowed, if the proper vouchers are presented. *Inspectors to render account to township board.*

(§58.) SEC. 6. The whole number of meetings of the township board of school inspectors at the expense of the township, during any one school year shall not exceed eight; but this shall not be construed to prevent said board holding further meetings in case of necessity, provided no expense to the township be incurred. *Number of meetings of inspectors.* *See App. A. ¶ 1.*

TOWNSHIP CLERK.

(§59.) SEC. 7. The township clerk shall be the clerk of the board of school inspectors by virtue of his office, and shall attend all meetings of said board, and, under their direction, prepare all their reports and record the same, and shall record all their proceedings. He shall also receive and keep all reports to inspectors from the directors of the several school districts in his township, and all the books and papers belonging to the inspectors, and file such papers in his office; and he shall receive all such communications, blanks, and documents as may be transmitted to him by the Superintendent of Public Instruction, and dispose of the same in the manner directed by said Superintendent. *Township clerk to be clerk of board of inspectors.* *See App. A, ¶¶ 163, 164.* *Duties as such.* *See §§ 142, 143.*

(§60.) SEC. 8. It shall be the duty of the township clerk annually, immediately after the organization of the board of school inspectors of his township, to transmit to the county clerk a certified statement of the name and post-office address of the chairman of said board; and in case there shall be a change in such chairman during the year, he shall immediately notify the county clerk of such change. *To notify county clerk of chairman of board of inspectors.*

(§61.) SEC. 9. Each township clerk shall cause a map to be made of his township, showing by distinct lines thereon the boundaries of each school district and parts of school *To make map of districts.*

districts therein, and shall regularly number the same
thereon as established by the inspectors. One copy of
such map shall be filed by the said clerk in his office,
and the other copy he shall file with the supervisor of
the township; and within one month after any division or
alteration of a district, or the organization of a new one
in his township, the said clerk shall file a new map and
copy thereof as aforesaid, showing the same.

Where map to
be filed.
When new map
to be made.

(§62.) SEC. 10. It shall be the duty of the township
clerk of each township, on or before the first day of
October of each year, to make and deliver to the supervisor of his township a certified copy of all statements
on file in his office of moneys proposed to be raised by
taxation in each of the several school districts of the
township for school purposes. He shall also certify to
the supervisor the amount to be assessed upon the taxable
property of any school district retaining the district schoolhouse or other property, on the division of the district, as
the same shall have been determined by the inspectors,
and he shall also certify the same to the director of such
district, and to the director of the district entitled thereto.

To report to
supervisor all
school taxes.
See § 146.
See App. B,
form 22.

(§63) SEC. 11. On receiving notice from the county
treasurer of the amount of school moneys apportioned to
his township, the township clerk shall apportion the same
amount to the several districts therein entitled to the same,
in proportion to the number of children in each between
the ages of five and twenty years, as the same shall be
shown by the annual report of the director of each district for the school year closing prior to the May apportionment.

To apportion
school moneys
received from
county treas-
urer.
See App. B,
form 20.

(§64.) SEC. 12. Said clerk shall also apportion to the
school districts in his township, as required by law, on
receiving notice of the amount from the township treasurer, all moneys raised by township tax, or received from
other sources, for the support of schools, and in all cases
make out and deliver to the township treasurer a written
statement of the number of children in each district drawing money, and the amount apportioned to each district,
and record the apportionment in his office; and whenever
an apportionment of the primary school interest fund, or
moneys raised by tax, or received from other sources, is
made, he shall give notice of the amount to be received
by each district to the director thereof.

To apportion
school taxes.
Statement to
township
treasurer.
See App. B,
forms 20, 21.
To notify direct-
ors of amount
apportioned to
districts.

TOWNSHIP SUPERVISOR AND TREASURER.

(§65.) SEC. 13. It shall be the duty of the supervisor
of the township to assess the taxes voted by every school
district in his township, and also all other taxes provided
for in this act, chargeable against such district or township, upon the taxable property of the district or township respectively, and to place the same on the township
assessment roll in the column for school taxes, and the

Assessment and
collection of
district taxes.
See § 146.

same shall be collected and returned by the township treasurer in the same manner and for the same compensation as township taxes. If any taxes provided for by law for school purposes shall fail to be assessed at the proper time, the same shall be assessed in the succeeding year. *Taxes not assessed at proper time.*

(§66.) SEC. 14. The supervisor shall also assess upon the taxable property of his township one mill upon each dollar of the valuation thereof in each year, and report the aggregate valuation of each district to the township clerk, who shall report said amount to the director of each school district in his township, or to the director of any fractional school district a portion of which may be located in said township, before the first day of September of each year; and all money so raised shall be apportioned by the township clerk to the district in which it was raised; and all money collected by virtue of this act during the year on any property not included in any organized district, or in districts not having, during the previous school year, three months' school in districts having less than thirty children, or five months' school in districts having thirty and less than eight hundred children, or nine months' school in districts having eight hundred or more children, as shown by the last school census, shall be apportioned to the several other school districts of said township, in the same manner as the primary school interest fund is now apportioned. All moneys accruing from the one mill tax in any township, before any district shall have a legal school therein, shall belong to the district in which it was raised, when they shall severally have had a three months' school by a qualified teacher. *Assessment of one-mill tax. How applied. When forfeited by districts. How apportioned. Where accrued moneys shall belong.*

(§67.) SEC. 15. The amount to be assessed upon the taxable property of any school district retaining the schoolhouse or other property, on the division of a district as the same shall have been determined by the inspectors, shall be assessed by the supervisor in the same manner as if the same had been authorized by a a vote of such *When district is divided certain taxes to be assessed.*

(§65.) A supervisor in levying school taxes erroneously included a part of the territory of one district in an adjoining district; and, when the tax was collected, it was paid to the district in which the supervisor had included the territory in question and not to the district in which the territory belonged. These proceedings on the part of the supervisor were clearly illegal, and the collection thereof could have been successfully resisted; or, if the taxes had been paid under protest, the parties paying could have recovered the amount thus unlawfully collected. It has been held by the Supreme Court that acquiescence in and payment of an illegal tax, estops the taxpayer from afterwards complaining of it; but the payment of an illegal tax, if refused, cannot be enforced—(Wattles vs. City of Lapeer, 40 Mich., 625. The People ex rel. Gebhart vs. East Saginaw, 30 Mich., 338). The taxes thus illegally assessed do not belong to either school district, therefore the one cannot sue the other for the recovery of such taxes improperly paid. It is not the money of the district in whose hands it now is, but it is an illegal tax collected from individuals, paid voluntarily and without protest, and therefore cannot be collected back; for the Supreme Court in the case cited (40 Mich., 625) says: "If the people taxed acquiesce and pay these taxes, they may not afterwards be heard to complain; but if they refuse, the courts have no power to compel them."—*Van Riper, Atty. Gen., July 24, 1882.*

(§66.) The only statute I notice relative to the assessment of school taxes is section 5090, Howell's statutes, and subsequent sections. They are to be assessed upon the taxable property of the districts or township. I suppose the personal property of residents of the district, together with the real estate of each resident within the district, would properly be taxed to each individual, notwithstanding the fact that some of his personal property was without the district and within the township. If the personalty was without the township and of that character to be assessable to another township another rule would apply. I do not think sections 10 and 11, Laws of 1885, applicable to school districts, or that they affect such taxes unless the property is in another township from where the party to be assessed resides.—*Taggart, Atty.Gen.*

district; and the money so assessed shall be placed to the credit of the taxable property taken from the former district, and shall be in reduction of any tax imposed in the new district on said taxable property for school district purposes: *Provided*, That if the district retaining the schoolhouse shall vote to pay and shall pay, before said taxes are assessed, any portion of said amount to the new district, said amount, as shall be certified by the moderator and director of the new district to the supervisor, shall be deducted from the amount to be assessed as provided in this section. When collected, such amount shall be paid over to the assessor of the new district, to be applied to the use thereof in the same manner, under the direction of its proper officers, as if such sum had been voted and raised by said district for building a schoolhouse or other district purposes.

Proviso.

How such taxes to be applied.

Taxes in fractional districts.

(§68.) Sec. 16. The full amount of all taxes to be levied upon the taxable property in a fractional school district shall be certified by the district board to the township clerk of each township in which such district is in part situated, and by such township clerks to the supervisors of their respective townships, and it shall be the duty of each of said supervisors to certify to each other supervisor interested, the amount of taxable property in that part of the district lying in his township: *Provided*, That when there exists a manifest difference in the valuation of property assessed in fractional districts composed of territory in adjoining townships or counties, such valuation shall be equalized for this specific purpose by the supervisors of the township interested, at a joint meeting held for that purpose, on application of either of the supervisors of said townships. And such supervisors shall respectively ascertain the proportion of such taxes, including mill tax, to be placed on their respective assessment rolls, according to the amount of taxable property in each part of such district. And if said supervisors cannot agree as to the proportion of such taxes to be placed on their respective assessment rolls, a supervisor from an adjoining township shall be called to meet with said supervisors in said fractional district and assist in equalizing said valuation, said supervisor to be paid at the rate of three dollars per diem for the time necessarily employed in attendance at such meeting of the supervisors, and all necessary traveling expenses by the townships in interest.

Proviso—how equalized.

Statement to township treasurer.

(§69.) Sec. 17. The supervisor, on delivery of the warrant for the collection of taxes to the township treasurer, shall also deliver to said treasurer, a written statement of the amount of school and library taxes, the amount raised for district purposes on the taxable property of each district in the township, the amount belonging to any new district on the division of the former district, and the names of all persons having judgments assessed under the provisions of this act upon the taxable property of any district, with the amount payable to such person on account thereof.

(§70.) Sec. 18. The supervisor of each township on the delivery of the warrant for the collection of taxes to the township treasurer, shall also deliver to said treasurer a written statement certified by him of the amount of the one-mill tax levied upon any property lying within the bounds of a fractional school district, a part of which is situate within his township and the returns of which are made to the clerk of some other township; and the said township treasurer shall pay to the township treasurer of such other township the amount of the taxes so levied and certified to him for the use of such fractional school district. *Statement to township treasurer of one-mill tax levied in fractional district.*

(§71.) Sec. 19. Whenever any portion of a school district shall be set off and annexed to any other district or organized into a new one, after a tax for district purposes other than the payment of any debts of the district shall have been levied upon the taxable property thereof but not collected, such tax shall be collected in the same manner as if no part of such district had been set off; and the said former district, and the district to which the portion so set off may be annexed, or the new district organized from such portion, shall each be entitled to such proportion of said tax as the amount of taxable property in each part thereof bears to the whole amount of taxable property on which such tax is levied. *Collection and apportionment of taxes on division of district.*

(§72.) Sec. 20. [Note.—Section 20 was repealed by Section 52 of Act number 206, Public Acts of 1893. See bottom of page.]

(§73) Sec. 21. The township treasurer shall, from time to time, apply to the county treasurer for all school and library moneys belonging to his township or the districts thereof; and on receipt of the moneys to be apportioned to the districts, he shall notify the township clerk of the amount to be apportioned. *Township treasurer to apply to county treasurer for moneys. See App. A, ¶¶ 144, 146. To notify township clerk of moneys.*

(§74.) Sec. 22. Each treasurer of a township, to the clerk of which the returns of any fractional school district shall be made, shall apply to the treasurer of any other township in which any part of such fractional school district may be situated, for any money to which such district may be entitled; and when so received it shall be certified to the township clerk, and apportioned in the same manner as other taxes for school purposes. *Moneys due fractional districts.*

(Section 52 of Act No. 206, Public Acts of 1893.) In case the township treasurer shall not collect the full amount of taxes required by his warrant to be paid into the township treasury, such portion thereof as he shall collect shall be retained by him to be paid out for the following purposes: The amount of school taxes collected to be paid on the order of the school district officers, the amount collected for general township purposes to be paid on the order of the township board, the amount collected for highway purposes to be paid on the order of the commissioner of highways countersigned by the township clerk or supervisor, and the amount collected for any special fund to be paid on the order of the proper officer; but in no case shall the amounts collected for any one fund be paid on the orders drawn on any other fund.

5

CHAPTER V.

COUNTY CLERK AND TREASURER.

County clerk to receive and dispose of communications, etc.

(§75.) SECTION 1. It shall be the duty of each county clerk to receive all such communications, blanks and documents as may be directed to him by the Superintendent of Public Instruction, and dispose of the same in the manner directed by said Superintendent.

County clerk to file inspectors' reports.

Notice of apportionment of moneys.

(§76.) SEC. 2. The clerk of each county shall, on receiving from the secretary of the county board of school examiners the annual reports of the several boards of school inspectors, file the same in his office. On receiving notice from the Superintendent of Public Instruction of the amount of moneys apportioned to the several townships in his county, he shall file the same in his office and forthwith deliver a copy thereof to the county treasurer.

County treasurer to apply for moneys appropriated.

To notify township clerks of amounts.

(§77.) SEC. 3. The several county treasurers shall apply for and receive such moneys as shall have been apportioned to their respective counties, when the same shall become due; and each of said treasurers shall immediately give notice to the treasurer and clerk of each township in his county, of the amount of school moneys apportioned to his township, and shall hold the same subject to the order of the township treasurer.

CHAPTER VI.

BONDED INDEBTEDNESS OF DISTRICTS.

Districts may borrow money and issue bonds.

Amount limited.

(§78.) SECTION 1. Any school district may, by a two-thirds vote of the qualified electors of said district present at any annual meeting, or a special meeting called for that purpose borrow money, and may issue bonds of the district therefor, to pay for a schoolhouse site or sites, and to erect and furnish school buildings as follows: Districts having less than thirty children between five and twenty years of age may have an indebtedness not to exceed three hundred dollars; districts having thirty children of like age may have an indebtedness not to exceed five hundred dollars; districts having fifty children of like age may have an indebtedness not to exceed one thousand dollars; districts having seventy-five children of like age may have an indebtedness not to exceed two thousand dollars; districts having one hundred children of like age may have an indebtedness not to exceed three thousand dollars; districts having one hundred twenty-five children of like age, and with an assessed valuation of not less than one hundred fifty thousand dollars, may have an indebtedness not to exceed five thousand dollars; districts having two hundred children of like age may have an indebtedness not to exceed eight thousand dollars; districts having three hundred children of like age may have an indebtedness not to exceed fifteen thousand dollars; districts having four hundred children of like age may have an indebtedness not to exceed twenty thousand dollars; districts having five hundred children of like age may have an indebtedness not to exceed twenty-five thousand dollars; and districts having eight hundred children or more of like age may have an indebtedness not to exceed thirty thousand dollars: *Provided*, That the indebtedness of a district shall in no case extend beyond ten years for money borrowed: *Provided further*, That in all proceedings under this section the director, assessor, and one person appointed by the district board shall constitute a board of inspection, who shall cause a poll list to be kept and a suitable ballot-box to be used, which shall be kept open two hours. The vote shall be by ballot either printed or written, or partly printed and partly written, and the canvass of the same shall be conducted in the same manner as at township elections or as the laws governing the same are applicable; and, when they are not, the board of inspectors shall prescribe the manner in which canvass shall be conducted. *(marginal note: Proviso—time for which bonds may be issued. Proviso—regulations at elections to issue bonds.)*

(§79.) SEC. 2. Whenever any school district shall have voted to borrow any sum of money, the district board of such district is hereby authorized to issue the bonds of such district in such form and executed in such manner by the moderator and director of such district, and in such sums, not less than fifty dollars, as such district board shall direct, and with such rate of interest, not exceeding eight per centum per annum and payable at such time or times as the said district shall have directed. *(marginal note: Issuing bonds for money borrowed. Interest thereon.)*

(§80.) SEC. 3. Whenever any money shall have been borrowed by any school district, the taxable inhabitants of such district are hereby authorized at any regular meeting of such district, to impose a tax on the taxable property in such district, for the purpose of paying the principal thus borrowed, or any part thereof and the interest thereon, to be levied and collected as other school district taxes are collected. *(marginal note: Voters may raise tax to redeem bonds.)*

(§81.) SEC. 4. Any school district, whenever it shall appear that the same can be done on terms advantageous to said district, may borrow money to pay any bonded indebtedness of said district then existing, and issue further bonds of said district therefor: *Provided*, That a majority of the qualified voters of said district shall so determine, at an annual or special meeting called for that purpose, and that the notice of such meeting, whether annual or special, shall state the intention to take such vote. *(marginal note: District may borrow money to pay bonds and issue further bonds. Proviso.)*

CHAPTER VII.

SUITS AND JUDGMENTS AGAINST DISTRICTS.

See App. A, ¶¶ 97, 109.

Justices to have jurisdiction in certain cases.

(§82.) SECTION 1. Justices of the peace shall have jurisdiction in all cases of assumpsit, debt, covenant, and trespass on the case against school districts, when the amount claimed or matter in controversy shall not exceed one hundred dollars; and the parties shall have the same right of appeal as in other cases.

Suit against district, how commenced.

(§83.) SEC. 2. When any suit shall be brought against a school district, it shall be commenced by summons, a copy of which shall be left with the assessor of the district at least eight days before the return day thereof.

No execution to issue against district.

(§84.) SEC. 3. No execution shall issue on any judgment against a school district, nor shall any suit be brought thereon, but the same shall be collected in the manner prescribed in this act.

Assessor to certify to supervisor's judgment against district.

(§85.) SEC. 4. Whenever any final judgment shall be obtained against a school district, if the same shall not be removed to any other court, the assessor of the district shall certify to the supervisor of the township and to the director of the district, the date and amount of such judgment, with the name of the person in whose favor the same was rendered; and if the judgment shall be removed to another court, the assessor shall certify the same as aforesaid, immediately after the final determination thereof against the district.

When assessor fails to certify, how party may proceed.

(§86.) SEC. 5. If the assessor shall fail to certify the judgment as required in the preceding section, it shall be lawful for the party obtaining the same, his executors, administrators, or assigns to file with the supervisor the certificate of the justice or clerk of the court rendering the judgment showing the facts which should have been certified by the assessor.

How judgment certified in case of fractional district.

(§87.) SEC. 6. If the district against whom any such judgment shall be rendered is situated in part in two or more townships, a certificate thereof shall be delivered as aforesaid to the supervisors of each township in which such district is in part situated.

Supervisors to assess amount of judgment.

(§88.) SEC. 7. The supervisor or supervisors receiving either of the certificates of a judgment as aforesaid shall proceed to assess the amount thereof, with interest from the date of the judgment to the time when the warrant for the collection thereof will expire, upon the taxable property of the district, placing the same on the next township assessment roll in the column for school taxes; and

How collected and returned.

the same proceedings shall be had, and the same shall be collected and returned, in the same manner as other district taxes.

CHAPTER VIII.

SITES FOR SCHOOLHOUSES.

(§89.) SECTION 1. The qualified voters of any school district, when lawfully assembled, may designate by a vote of two-thirds of those present, such number of sites as may be desired for schoolhouses, and may change the same by a similar vote at any annual meeting. When no site can be established by such inhabitants as aforesaid, the school inspectors of the township or townships in which the district is situated shall determine where such site shall be, and their determination shall be certified to the director of the district, and shall be final, subject to alteration afterward by the inspectors, on the written request of two-thirds of the qualified voters of the district, or by two-thirds of the qualified voters agreeing upon a site, at a district meeting lawfully called.

(§90.) SEC. 2. Whenever a site for a schoolhouse shall be designated, determined, or established in any manner provided by law, in any school district, and such district shall be unable to agree with the owner or owners of such site upon the compensation to be paid therefor, or in case such district shall, by reason of any imperfection in the title to said site, arising either from break in the chain of title, tax sale, mortgages, levies, or any other cause, be unable to procure a perfect, unincumbered title, in fee simple to said site, the district board of such district shall authorize one or more of its members to apply to the circuit judge, if there be one in the county, or to a circuit court commissioner of the county, or to any justice of the peace of the city or township in which such school district shall be situated, for a jury to ascertain and determine the just compensation to be made for the real estate required by such school district for such site, and the necessity for using the same, which application shall be in writing and shall describe the real estate required by such district as accurately as is required in a conveyance of real estate: *Provided*, That whenever any school district shall have designated, selected, or established, in any manner provided by law, a schoolhouse site, such selection, designation, or establishment shall be *prima facie* evidence to said jury of the necessity to use the site so established.

(§91.) SEC. 3. It shall be the duty of such circuit judge, circuit court commissioner, or justice of the peace, upon such application being made to him, to issue a summons, or *venire*, directed to the sheriff or any constable of the county, commanding him to summon eighteen freeholders residing in the vicinity of such site, who are in no wise of kin to the owner of such real estate and not interested therein, to appear before such judge, commissioner, or justice, at the time and place therein named, not less than

Marginal notes: See App. A, ¶¶ 114, 124. Voters to designate sites. When inspectors shall determine site. See App. B, form 17. Disagreement upon compensation for site. Board to apply for a jury. Contents of application. Proviso—evidences of necessity for site. Jury to be summoned.

twenty nor more than fifty days from the time of issuing such summons, or *venire*, as a jury to ascertain and determine the just compensation to be made for the real estate required by such school district for such site, and the **Owner to be notified.** necessity for using the same, and to notify the owner or occupant of such real estate, if he can be found in the county, of the time when and the place where such jury is summoned to appear, and the object for which such jury is summoned, which notice shall be served at least ten days before the time specified in such summons, or *venire*, for the jury to appear as hereinbefore mentioned.

Notice in case owner is unknown, etc. (§92.) SEC. 4. Thirty days' previous notice of the time when and the place where such jury will assemble shall be given by the district board of such district, where the owner or owners of such real estate shall be unknown, non-residents of the county, minors, insane, *non compos mentis*, or inmates of any prison, by publishing the same in a newspaper published in the county where such real estate is situated; or, if there be no newspaper published in such county, then in some newspaper published in the nearest county where a newspaper is published, once in each week for four successive weeks, which notice shall be signed by the district board or by the director or assessor of such district, and shall describe the real estate required for such site, and state the time when and place where such jury will assemble and the object for which they will assemble; or such notice may be served on such owner personally, or by leaving a copy thereof at his last place of residence.

Return of *venire* and proceedings thereon. (§93.) SEC. 5. It shall be the duty of such judge, commissioner, or justice, and of the persons summoned as jurors, as hereinbefore provided, and of the sheriff or constable summoning them, to attend at the time and place specified in such summons, or *venire;* and the officer who summoned the jury shall return such summons, or *venire*, to the officer who issued the same, with the names of the persons summoned by him as jurors, and shall certify the manner of notifying the owner or owners of such real estate, if he was found; and if he could not be found in said county, he shall certify that fact. Either party may challenge any of the said jurors for the same causes as in civil actions. If more than twelve of said jurors in attendance shall be found qualified to serve as jurors, the officers in attendance and who issued the summons, or *venire*, for such jury, shall strike from the list of jurors a number sufficient to reduce the number of jurors in attendance to twelve; and in case less than twelve of the number so summoned as jurors shall attend, the sheriff or constable shall summon a sufficient number of freeholders to make up the number of twelve; and the officer issuing the sum- **Attachment may issue to enforce obedience to process.** mons, or *venire*, for such jury may issue an attachment for any persons summoned as a juror who shall fail to attend, and may enforce obedience to such summons, *venire*, or attachment, as courts of record or justices' courts are authorized to do in civil cases.

(§94.) SEC. 6. The twelve persons selected as the jury shall be duly sworn by the judge, commissioner, or justice in attendance, faithfully and impartially to inquire, ascertain, and determine the just compensation to be made for the real estate required by such school district for such site, and the necessity for using the same in the manner proposed by such school district; and the persons thus sworn shall constitute the jury in such case. Subpœnas for witnesses may be issued, and their attendance compelled by such circuit judge, commissioner, or justice in the same manner as may be done by the circuit court or by a justice's court in civil cases. The jury may visit and examine the premises and, from such examination and such other evidences as may be presented before them, shall ascertain and determine the necessity for using such real estate in the manner and for the purpose proposed by such school district, and the just compensation to be made therefore; and if such jury shall find that it is necessary that such real estate shall be used in the manner or for the purpose proposed by such school district, they shall sign a certificate in writing, stating that it is necessary that said real estate, describing it, should be used as a site for a schoolhouse for such district, also stating the sum to be paid by such school district as the just compensation for the same. The said circuit judge, circuit court commissioner, or justice of the peace, shall sign and attach to, and endorse upon the certificate thus subscribed by the said jurors, a certificate stating the time when and the place where the said jury assembled, that they were by him duly sworn as herein required, and that they subscribed the said certificate. He shall also state in such certificate who appeared for the respective parties on such hearing and inquiry, and shall deliver such certificates to the director or to any member of the district board of such school district.

Jury to be sworn.

Subpœnas for witnesses.

Jury to ascertain necessity for taking land.

To determine compensation therefor.

Court to make certificate.

(§95.) SEC. 7. Upon filing such certificates in the circuit court of the county where such real estate is situated, such court shall, if it finds all the proceedings regular, render judgment for the sum specified in the certificate signed by such jury, against such school district, which judgment shall be collected and paid in the manner as other judgments against school districts are collected and paid.

Collection of judgment.

(§96.) SEC. 8. In case the owner of such real estate shall be unknown, insane, *non compos mentis*, or an infant, or cannot be found within such county, it shall be lawful for the said school district to deposit the amount of such judgment with the county treasurer of such county, for the use of the person or persons entitled thereto; and it shall be the duty of such county treasurer to receive such money, and at the time of receiving it, to give a receipt or certificate to the person depositing the same with him,

When owner is unknown, etc., money to be deposited with county treasurer may be drawn.

stating the time when such deposit was made, and for what
purpose; and such county treasurer and his sureties shall
be liable on his bond for any money which shall come
into his hands under the provisions of this act, in case
he shall refuse to pay or account for the same, as herein
required: *Provided*, That no such money shall be drawn
from such county treasurer, except upon an order of the
circuit court, circuit court commissioner, or judge of probate, as hereinafter provided.

Proviso—how money to be drawn from county treasurer.

(§97.) SEC. 9. Upon satisfactory evidence being presented
to the circuit court of the county where such real estate
lies, that such judgment or the sum ascertained and determined by the jury as the just compensation to be paid
by such district for such site, has been paid, or that the
amount thereof has been deposited according to the provisions of the preceding sections, such court shall, by an
order or decree, adjudge and determine that the title in
fee of such real estate shall, from the time of making
such payment or deposit, forever thereafter be vested in
such school district and its successors and assigns, and
shall, in and by such order or decree, award to such school
district a writ of possession for the recovery of the possession of such real estate; a copy of which order or
decree, certified by the clerk of said county, shall be
recorded in the office of the register of deeds of such
county, and the title of such real estate shall thenceforth,
from the time of making such payment or deposit, be
vested forever thereafter in such school district and its
successors and assigns in fee.

On payment court to decree title vested in district.

Copy of decree to be recorded.

(§98.) SEC. 10. Such school district may, at any time
after making payment or deposit hereinbefore required,
enter upon and take possession of such real estate for the
use of said district. And it shall be the duty of the
county clerk of said county, on the request of said school
district, to issue out of and under the seal of the circuit
court of said county, a writ of possession as awarded in
such order or decree, which writ shall be directed to the
sheriff of said county, and shall be tested and made
returnable, and shall be substantially, so far as may be,
in the same form provided for writs of possession in
actions of ejectment; and it shall be the duty of such
sheriff thereupon to remove the respondent or respondents
in such proceedings, and all persons holding under them
or either of them, from the real estate described in such
decree and in such writ, and deliver the possession thereof
with the appurtenances to such school district.

When district to take possession.

Writ of possession to be issued by county clerk to sheriff.

Sheriff to remove respondent.

(§99.) SEC. 11. In case the jury hereinbefore provided
for shall not agree, another jury may be summoned in the
same manner, and the same proceedings may be had,
except that no further notice of the proceedings shall be
necessary; but instead of such notice, the judge, commissioner, or justice may adjourn the proceedings to such time
as he shall think reasonable, not exceeding thirty days, and

When jury disagrees, proceedings may be adjourned and new jury summoned.

shall make the process to summon a jury returnable at such time and place as the said proceedings shall be adjourned to. Such proceedings may be adjourned from Adjournments not to exceed three months. time to time by the said judge, or commissioner, or justice, on the application of either party and for good cause, to be shown by the party applying for such adjournment, unless the other party shall consent to such adjournment; but such adjournment shall not in all exceed three months.

(§100.) SEC. 12. In case the said schoolhouse site is Proceedings in case of incumbrances. encumbered by mortgage, levy, tax sale or otherwise, as aforesaid, the mortgagee or other parties claiming to be interested in said title shall severally be made a party to the procedure as aforesaid, and shall be authorized, upon the filing of the certificate of the jury in the circuit court of said county, to appear before the circuit judge and make proof relative to their proportionate claims to the said site, or the compensation to be made therefor as determined by said jury. And the said circuit judge shall, Duty of circuit judge. by decree, settle their several claims in accordance with the rights of the parties respectively, and may divide the sum awarded by said jury between the claimants as in his judgment will be equitable and right, rendering against said district a separate judgment for each of the amounts so awarded.

(§101.) SEC. 13. The circuit judge, judge of probate, or How money deposited with county treasurer may be drawn. circuit court commissioner of any county where any money has been deposited with the county treasurer of such county, as hereinbefore provided, shall, upon the written application of any person or persons entitled to such money, and upon receiving satisfactory evidence of the right of such applicant to the money thus deposited, make an order directing the county treasurer to pay the money thus deposited with him to said applicant; and it shall be the duty of such county treasurer, on the presentation of such order, with the receipt of the person named therein indorsed on said order and duly acknowledged, in the same manner as conveyances of real estate are required to be acknowledged, to pay the same; and such order, with the receipt of the applicant or person in whose favor the same shall be drawn, shall, in all courts and places, be presumptive evidence in favor of such county treasurer, to exonerate him from all liability to any person or persons for said money thus paid by him.

(§102.) SEC. 14. Circuit judges, circuit court commis- Compensation of officers on proceedings. sioners, and justices of the peace, for any services rendered under the provisions of this act, shall be entitled to the same fees and compensation as for similar services in other special proceedings. Jurors, constables, and sheriffs shall be entitled to the same fees as for like services in civil cases in the circuit court.

(§103.) SEC. 15. In case any circuit judge, circuit court When judge, etc., unable to attend, another may finish proceedings. commissioner, or justice of the peace, who shall issue a

6

summons, or *venire*, for a jury, shall be unable to attend to any of the subsequent proceedings in such case, any other circuit court commissioner or justice of the peace may attend and finish said proceedings.

CHAPTER IX.

APPEALS FROM ACTION OF INSPECTORS.

(§104.) SECTION 1. Whenever any five or more tax paying electors, having taxable property within any school district, shall feel themselves aggrieved by any action, order, or decision of the board of school inspectors, with reference to the formation, or any division, or consolidation of said school district, they may, at any time within sixty days from the time of such action on the part of said school inspectors, appeal from such action, order, or decision of said board of school inspectors to the township board of the township in which such school district is situated; and

in case of fractional school districts notice of such appeal shall be served on the clerk of the joint boards of school inspectors who have made the decision appealed from, who shall, within five days, give notice thereof to the township boards of the several townships in which the different parts of said fractional school district are situated, who

shall have power and whose duty it shall be, acting jointly, to entertain such appeal, and review, confirm, set aside, or amend the action, order, or decision of the board of school inspectors thus appealed from; or if in their opinion the appeal is frivolous or without sufficient cause, they may summarily dismiss the same.

(§105.) SEC. 2. Said appellants shall, before taking such appeal, make out and file with the board of school inspectors, or in case of fractional school districts, to the clerk of the joint boards of school inspectors, a written statement to be signed by said appellants, setting forth in general terms the action, order, or decision of the board or boards of school inspectors with respect to which the appellants feel themselves aggrieved, and their demand for an appeal therefrom to the township board or boards of

said township or townships, and shall also cause to be executed and signed by one of their number, and by two good and sufficient sureties, to be approved by the clerk of said board or joint boards of school inspectors or by

any justice of the peace of the township, and file with the clerk of said board or joint boards of school inspectors, a bond to the people of the State of Michigan in the penal sum of two hundred dollars, conditioned for the due prosecution of said appeal before said township board or boards acting jointly, and also, in case of the dismissal of said appeal as frivolous by said township board or joint boards, for the payment by said appellants of all costs occasioned to the township or townships by reason of said appeal.

(§106.) SEC. 3. Upon the filing of such appeal, papers and bond with the said board or joint boards of school inspectors, the said board or joint boards of school inspectors shall, within ten days thereafter, make out and file with the clerk of said township in which the said schoolhouse is located, a full and complete transcript of all their proceedings, actions, orders, or decisions, with reference to which the appeal is taken, and of their records of the same, also said bond and appeal papers, and all petitions and remonstrances, if any, with reference to the matters appealed from; and upon the filing of the same with the said township clerk, the said township board or boards shall be deeemd to be in possesson of the case, and if the return be deemed by them insufficient, may order a further and more complete return by said board or boards of school inspectors; and when such return shall by them be deemed sufficient, they shall proceed with the consideration of the appeal, at such time or times, within ten days after such return, and in such manner and under such affirmation, amendment or reversal of the action, order, or decision of the board or boards of school inspectors appealed from, as in their judgment shall seem to be just and right; or, if they deem the appeal to be frivolous, they may summarily dismiss the same; but the decision of said board or boards of school inspectors shall not be altered or reversed, unless a majority of such township board or boards, not members of said board or boards of school inspectors, shall so determine.

Duty of inspectors when appeal is filed.

When township board deemed in possession of case.

Proceedings in the appeal.

When members of township board cannot act in determining case. See App. A, ¶¶ 14, 15.

CHAPTER X.

GRADED SCHOOL DISTRICTS.

(§107.) SECTION 1. Any school district containing more than one hundred children between the ages of five and twenty years may, by a two-thirds vote of the qualified electors present at any annual or special meeting, organize as a graded school district: *Provided*, That the intention

See App. A, ¶¶ 135, 143.

What districts may organize as such.

Proviso, notice of meeting.

(§107.) Elections held in graded school districts wherein two trustees were balloted for at the same time, on joint ballot, are void, and no person has been legally elected. It has frequently been held that, if a ballot contains the names of two persons for the same office, when but one is to be chosen, it is bad as to both. The election of two trustees on two separate ballots, would be good as to the first one chosen, and void as to the second. As it is the policy of the law to uphold elections where the choice of the people can be ascertained, the one first elected having received the necessary vote is the choice of the electors, and such action of the district is valid as to him. As the amendment of 1883 does not repeal Section 1, Act X, only so far as it is in conflict therewith, and as both statutes provide that trustees shall hold over until their successors shall be elected and qualified, the old board remain in office until a valid election is had. The law makes no provision for a special election for trustees of graded schools, hence where the regular election was void there can be no special election to fill the office. No election can be held without a law providing therefor, hence the law that both trustees hold over is in full force whenever there was a failure to elect, as provided by statute. Section 2, chapter 3, of the school law applies only to officers of district schools and not to trustees of graded schools, and only permits a special election where two vacancies exist. The trustees have no power under Section 2, chapter X, to appoint a trustee where there has been a failure to elect, but can only fill vacancies, as in case of death, resignation, or removal.—*Van Riper, Atty. Gen., July 26, 1883.*

to take such vote shall be expressed in the notice of such annual or special meeting. When such change in the organization of the district shall have been voted, the voters at such annual or special meeting shall proceed immediately to elect by ballot from the qualified voters of the district one trustee for the term of one year, two for the term of two years, and two for a term of three years, and annually thereafter a successor or successors to the trustee or trustees whose term of office shall expire: *Provided also,* In all districts organized prior to the year eighteen hundred eighty-three, there shall be one trustee elected at the annual meeting for the year eighteen hundred eighty-three, and thereafter there shall be elected a trustee or trustees in the manner aforesaid, whose term of office shall be three years and until his or their successor or successors shall have been elected and filed his or their acceptance: *Provided also,* That in the election of trustees and all other school officers, the person receiving a majority of all the votes shall be declared elected.

(§108.) SEC. 2. Within ten days after their election such trustees shall file with the director acceptances of the offices to which they have been elected, and shall annually elect from their own number a moderator, a director, and assessor, and for cause may remove the same, and may appoint others of their own number in their places, who shall perform the duties prescribed by law for such officers in other school districts in this State, except as hereinafter provided. The trustees shall have power to fill any vacancy that may occur in their number, till the next annual meeting. Whenever, in any case, the trustees shall fail, through disagreement or neglect, to elect the officers named in this section, within twenty days next after the annual meeting, the school inspectors of the township or city to which such district makes its annual report shall appoint the said officers from the number of said trustees.

(§109.) SEC. 3. It shall be the duty of the board of trustees of any graded school district:

First, To classify and grade the pupils attending school in such district, and cause them to be taught in such schools or departments as they may deem expedient;

Second, To establish in such district a high school, when ordered by a vote of the district at an annual meeting, and to determine the qualifications for admission to such school and the fees to be paid for tuition in any branches taught therein: *Provided,* That when non-resident pupils, their parents, or guardians, shall pay a school tax in said

---

(§109, ¶ 4.) The question is as to whether the board of trustees of a graded school can employ a music teacher who has not passed the regular examination required of other teachers and received a certificate required by section 5153 of Howell's Statutes (Sec. 4, Chap. 11, School Laws)? It would be most difficult to imagine that an examination in the several branches and studies specified in the statutes would show sufficiently the qualifications of the applicants to teach either music or drawing. I do not think the statutes applicable to such teachers, nor does there appear to be any which is. The board probably has and will be held by the courts to possess such authority, still it is not a question free from doubt, and additional legislation may be desirable.—*Taggart, Attorney General, July 26, 1886.*

district, the same shall be credited on their tuition a sum not to exceed the amount of such tuition; and they shall only be required to pay tuition for the difference between the amount of the tax and the amount charged for tuition;

Third, To audit and order the payment of all accounts of the director for incidental or other expenses incurred by him in the discharge of his duties; but no more than fifty dollars shall be expended by the director in any one year for repairs of the buildings or appurtenances of the district property, without the authority of the board of trustees; ^{To audit and pay director's accounts.}

Fourth, To employ all qualified teachers necessary for the several schools, and to determine the amount of their compensation, and to require the director and moderator to make contracts with the same on behalf of the district, in accordance with the provisions of law concerning contracts with teachers; ^{To employ teachers. See § 40. See App. B, form 26. See App. A. ¶¶ 70-86.}

Fifth, To employ such officers and servants as may be necessary for the management of the schools and school property, and prescribe their duties and fix their compensation; ^{To employ officers, etc.}

Sixth, To perform such other duties as are required of district boards in other school districts; ^{Other duties. See Chap. III.}

(§110.) SEC. 4. No alteration shall be made in the boundaries of any graded school district, without the consent of a majority of the trustees of said district, which consent shall be spread upon the records of the district and placed on file in the office of the clerk of the board of school inspectors of the township or city to which the reports of said district are made; and graded school districts shall not be restricted to nine sections of land. ^{Consent of trustees necessary to change in boundaries of districts.} ^{Such districts not restricted in size.}

(§111.) SEC. 5. Whenever two or more contiguous districts having together more than one hundred children between the ages of five and twenty years, after having published in the notices of the annual meetings of each district the intention to take such action, shall severally, by a vote of two-thirds of the qualified voters attending the annual meetings in said districts, determine to unite for the purpose of establishing a graded school district under the provisions of this chapter, the school inspectors of the township or townships in which such districts may be situated shall, on being properly notified of such vote, proceed to unite such districts, and shall appoint, as soon as practicable, a time and place for a meeting of the new district, and shall require three notices of the same to be posted in each of the districts so united, at least five days before the time of such meeting; and at such meeting the district shall elect a board of trustees, as provided in section one of this chapter, and may do whatever business may be done at any annual meeting. ^{Two or more districts can unite and form graded school district.} ^{Notice of meeting.}

(§112.) SEC. 6. Whenever the trustees of any organized graded school district shall be presented twenty days before the annual meeting thereof, with a petition signed by ten ^{Duty of trustees in certain cases, etc.}

electors of said district, stating that it is the desire of said petitioners that, at the annual meeting of said school district, there shall be submitted to said annual meeting the proposition to change from a graded school district to one or more primary school districts, the said trustees shall, *In case of vote to change from graded school district to primary.* in their notice of such annual meeting, state that the proposition set forth in said petition will be presented to said meeting; and if two-thirds of the qualified voters present at said meeting shall vote to change to one or more primary school districts, such change shall be made: and it shall be the duty of the board of school inspectors of the township or townships in which such district is situated, upon being duly notified of such vote, to proceed to change or divide such district as determined by such annual meeting, and they shall provide for the holding of the first meeting in the or each of the proposed primary school districts in the same manner as is provided for by law for the organization of primary school districts; and whenever a fractional graded school district shall be so changed, the township boards of school inspectors of the respective townships where such graded school district is situated, shall organize the said district into one or more primary school districts, as provided by law.

CHAPTER XI.

LIBRARIES.

Township libraries to be maintained. (§113.) SECTION 1. A township library shall be maintained in each organized township, which shall be the property of the township, and shall not be subject to sale or alienation from any cause whatever. All actions relating to such library or for the recovery of any penalties lawfully established in relation thereto, shall be brought in the name of the township.

Who are entitled to privileges of library. (§114.) SEC. 2. All persons who are residents of the township shall be entitled to the privileges of the township library, subject to such rules and regulations as may *Proviso.* be lawfully established in relation thereto: *Provided,* That persons residing within the boundaries of any school district in which a district library has been established shall be entitled to the privileges of such district library only.

Inspectors to have charge. *See App. B, form 18.* *See App. A, ¶¶ 144, 146.* (§115.) SEC. 3. The township board of school inspectors shall have charge of the township library, and shall apply for and receive from the township treasurer all moneys appropriated for the township library of their township, and shall purchase the books and procure the necessary appendages for such library.

Inspectors accountable for care, etc., of library. *Powers of inspectors.* (§116.) SEC. 4. Said board shall be held accountable for the proper care and preservation of the township library, and shall have power to provide for the safe keeping of the same, to prescribe the time for taking and returning

books, to assess and collect fines and penalties for the loss See App. C.
or injury of said books, and to establish all other needful
rules and regulations for the management of the library,
as said board shall deem proper or the Superintendent of
Public Instruction may advise.

(117.) SEC. 5. The board of school inspectors shall cause Where library to be kept.
the township library to be kept at some central or eligible
place in the township, which it shall determine; such board Librarian.
shall also, within ten days after the annual township meeting, appoint a librarian for the term of one year, to have
the care and superintendence of said library, who shall be
responsible to the board of school inspectors for the impar-
tial enforcement of all rules and regulations lawfully established in relation to said library.

(§118.) SEC. 6. Any school district, by a two-thirds vote What districts may establish libraries.
at any annual meeting, may establish a district library;
and such district shall be entitled to its just proportion
of books from the library of any township in which it is
wholly or partly situated, to be added to the district
library, and also to its equitable share of any library
moneys remaining unexpended in any such township or
townships at the time of the establishment of such district
library, or that shall thereafter be raised by tax in such
township or townships, or that shall thereafter be apportioned to the township to the inspectors of which the
annual report of its director is made.

(§119.) SEC. 7. The district board of any school district District board to have charge of district library.
in which a district library may be established in accord-
ance with the provisions of this act, shall have charge of
such library; and the duties and responsibilities of said
district board in relation to the district library, and all
moneys raised or apportioned for its support, shall be the
same as those of the board of school inspectors are to the
township library.

(§120.) SEC. 8. The school inspectors shall give in their Inspectors to report library statistics to State superin-tendent.
annual report to the Superintendent of Public Instruction
such facts and statistics relative to the management of the
township library and the library moneys, as the Superintendent of Public Instruction shall direct; and the district
board of any school district having a library shall cause
to be given in the annual report of the director to the
board of school inspectors, like facts and statistics relative
to the district library, which items shall also be included
by the said inspectors in their annual report.

(§121.) SEC. 9. In case the board of school inspectors Failure to re-port or illegal use of moneys to cause forfeiture of moneys there-after.
of any township or the district board of any school dis-
trict, shall fail to make the report required by the preceding section, or in case it shall appear from the reports so
made that any township or school district has failed to
use the library money in strict accordance with the provisions of law, such township or district shall forfeit its
share of the library moneys that are apportioned; and the
same shall be apportioned to the several other townships

Proviso. and districts in the county as hereinafter provided: *Provided,* That in townships where the boards thereof shall determine and report to the superintendent that the public will be better served by using the said money for general school purposes, no such forfeiture shall occur.

State superintendent to provide county clerk with statement. (§122.) SEC. 10. The Superintendent of Public Instruction shall annually and previous to the tenth day of May, transmit to the clerk of each county a statement of the townships in his county that are entitled to receive library moneys, giving the number of children in each of such townships between the ages of five and twenty years, as shall appear from the reports of the boards of school **Statement to be filed and copy given to county treasurer.** inspectors for the school year last ending; said clerk shall file such statement in his office, and shall forthwith furnish a copy thereof to the county treasurer.

Apportionment of proceeds of penal fines. (§123.) SEC. 11. The clear proceeds of all fines for any breach of the penal laws of this State and for penalties, or upon any recognizance in criminal proceedings, and all **See App. A, ¶ 140.** equivalents for exemptions [exemption] from military duty, when collected in any county and paid into the county treasury, together wth all moneys heretofore collected and paid into said treasury on account of such fines or equiv- **How applied.** alents, and not already appropriated [apportioned], shall be apportioned by the county treasurer before the first day of June in each year, among the several townships in the county, according to the number of children therein between the ages of five and twenty years, as shown by the statement of the Superintendent of Public Instruction provided for in the preceding section, which money shall be exclusively applied to the support* of the township and district libraries, and to no other purpose.

Voters may levy tax for support of libraries. (§124.) SEC. 12. The qualified voters of each township shall have power at any annual township meeting, to vote a tax for the support of libraries established in accordance with the provisions of this act; and the qualified voters of any school district in which a district library shall be established, shall have power at any annual meeting of such district, to vote a district tax for the support of said **How tax to be reported, assessed, and collected.** district library. When any tax authorized by this section shall have been voted, it shall be reported to the supervisor, levied, and collected in the same manner as other township and school district taxes.

District board may give or sell books to township library. (§125.) SEC. 13. The district board of any school district may donate or sell any library book or books belonging to such district, to the board of school inspectors of the township or townships in which said district is wholly or partly situated, which book or books shall thereafter form a part of the township library.

* Amended by Act No. 15, Public Acts of 1895.

CHAPTER XII.

Act No. 147, Public Acts of 1891, as amended by Act No. 34, Public Acts of 1893, and by
Act No. 66, Public Acts of 1895.

EXAMINATION OF TEACHERS AND SUPERVISION OF SCHOOLS.

(§126.) SECTION 1. At the meetings of the several boards _{First appoint-} of supervisors of the different counties of the State to be _{sioner of schools.} held on the fourth Monday in June, eighteen hundred ninety-one, the said several boards of supervisors shall elect a county commissioner of schools for their respective counties, whose term of office shall commence on the fourth. Tuesday of August next following, who shall hold his or her office until the first day of July, eighteen hundred ninety-three, or until his or her successor shall be elected and qualified. Said board of supervisors shall also _{Appointment of examiner.} on said fourth Monday of June, appoint two persons as school examiners, who, together with said commissioner of schools, shall constitute a board of school examiners. One of said school examiners shall be appointed for a period of one year and the other for a period of two years, from and after the second Monday of October next after their appointment, or until their successors have been appointed and qualified. And thereafter such boards of supervisors _{Term of examiner.} shall, at each annual session, appoint one examiner who shall hold his office for a period of two years, or until his successor shall have been appointed and qualified. Any _{Qualifications of examiner.} person shall be eligible to the office of examiner who shall hold at least a third grade certificate and has taught in the public schools at least nine months, or who has the qualifications required of commissioners in section three of this act, except an experience of twelve months as teacher. In case a vacancy shall occur at any time in the _{Vacancy.} office of school examiner, the judge of probate, together with the board of school examiners of the county in which such vacancy shall have occurred, shall within ten days after the occurrence of such vacancy, appoint some suitable person to fill such vacancy; and the person so appointed shall hold the office for the unexpired portion of the term, or until his or her successor is appointed and has qualified. Within ten days after such commissioners or _{Official bond.} examiners shall have received legal notice of his or her election, he or she shall take and subscribe the constitutional oath of office, and the same shall be filed with the county clerk. The said county commissioner so appointed, shall execute a bond with two sufficient sureties, to be approved by and filed with the county clerk, in the penal sum of one thousand dollars, conditioned that he or she shall faithfully discharge the duties of his or her office according to law, and to faithfully account for and pay

7

over to the proper persons all money which may come into his or her hands by reason of his or her holding such office; and thereupon the county clerk shall report the name and postoffice address of such county commissioner to the State Superintendent of Public Instruction.

Biennial election of commissioner. (§127.) SEC. 2. There shall be elected at the election held on the first Monday in April, eighteen hundred ninety-three and every second year thereafter, in each county, one *Term of office.* county commissioner of schools whose term of office shall commence on the first day of July next following his or her election, and ·who shall continue in office two years or until his or her successor shall be elected and qualified. The county commissioner of schools elected under the pro-
To file oath and bond. visions of this section shall file with the county clerk for the county for which he or she is elected, his or her oath of office and bond, the same as provided in section one of this act, and the county clerk shall make the same report to the Superintendent of Public Instruction in all respects as provided in section one of this act.

Eligibility to office of, etc. (§128.) SEC. 3. Persons eligible to hold the office of commissioner of schools must· possess, besides an experience *See App. A, ¶¶ 168-170.* of twelve months as teacher in the public schools of the State, one of the following qualifications; must be a graduate of the literary department of some reputable college, university, or State normal school, having a course of at least three years, or hold a State teachers' certificate, or be the holder of a first grade certificate; but said first grade certificate shall only qualify the holder thereof to hold the office of commissioner in the county where such certificate *Proviso as to certain counties.* was granted: *Provided,* That persons who have held the office of commissioner of schools under the provisions of act number one hundred forty-seven, public acts of eighteen hundred ninety-one, shall be eligible. In counties having less than fifty districts subject to the supervision of the county commissioner, a person holding at the time of his or her election a second grade certificate shall be eligible.

Schedule of examinations. (§129.) SEC. 4. The board of school examiners shall, for the purpose of examining all persons who may offer themselves as teachers for the public schools, hold two regular public examinations. in each year at the county seat, which examinations shall begin on the last Thursday of March and the third Thursday of August in each year. From these two examinations certificates of all grades may be granted. The said board of examiners may also in their discretion hold two other regular public examinations, which shall begin on the third Thursdays of June and October at such places as in the judgment of the board the best interests of the teachers may require. From these two examinations only certificates of the second and third grades may be granted.

In counties having one hundred fifty or more districts, the said board of examiners may hold one special public

examination for each additional twenty-five districts or Counties entitled to more than four examinations.
fractions thereof, which special public examination, when
appointed, shall be held commencing on one or more of
the following dates: the third Friday of February, April See App. A,
and September. The place of holding such special public ¶¶ 79-96,
examination is also left to the discretion of the board of ¶¶ 166-167.
examiners. At such special public examinations only cer- See §§ 217, 167, 169.
tificates of the third grade shall be granted. It shall be
the duty of the county commissioner to make out a schedule of the times and places of holding special examinations, and to cause it to be published in one or more
newspapers of the county at least ten days before each
special examination.

(§130.) SEC. 5. The board of school examiners shall Granting of certificates.
meet on the Saturday of the week following such public
examination held by the county commissioner, and shall
grant certificates· to teachers in such form as the Superintendent of Public Instruction shall prescribe, licensing as
teachers all persons who shall have attained the age of
seventeen years who have attended such public examinations and who shall be found qualified in respect to good
moral character, learning, and ability to instruct and govern
a school; but no certificate shall be granted to any person
who, having arrived at the age of twenty-one years, is not a
citizen of the United States, and who shall not have passed
a satisfactory examination in orthography, reading, writing,
grammar, geography, arithmetic, theory and art of teaching,
United States history, civil government, and physiology
and hygiene, with reference to the effect of alcoholic drinks,
stimulants, and narcotics upon the human system. The
board of examiners shall have the right, however, to renew
without examination the certificates of persons who shall
have previously obtained an average standing of at least
eighty-five per cent in all studies covered in two or more
previous examinations, and who shall have been since such
last named examination continuously and successfully teaching in the same county. All certificates shall be signed By whom signed.
by the county commissioner and by at least one other
member of the board of examiners. No person shall be
considered a qualified teacher within the meaning of this
act, nor shall any school officer employ or contract with
any person to teach in any of the public schools under the
provisions of this act, who has not a certificate in force
granted by the board of school examiners or other lawful
authority. All examination questions shall be prepared and Examination questions.
furnished by the Superintendent of Public Instruction to
the county commissioner under seal, to be opened in the
presence of the applicants for certificates on the day of
examination.

(§131.) SEC. 6. There shall be three grades of certifi- Grades of certificates.
cates granted by the board of school examiners, in its discretion, and subject to such rules and regulations as the
Superintendent of Public Instruction may prescribe, which

grades of certificates shall be as follows: The certificate of the first grade shall be granted only to those who have taught at least one year with ability and success, and it Proviso. shall be valid throughout the State for four years: *Provided*, That all examination papers for first grade certificates favorably passed upon by the board of examiners, together with such certificates, shall be forwarded to the Superintendent of Public Instruction within ten days from *Further proviso.* date of examination, for inspection: *And provided further*, That no first grade certificate shall be valid in any county other than that in which it is granted, unless approved and countersigned by the Superintendent of Public Instruction, and a copy filed with the county commissioner in the county in which the holder of said certificate desires *Second grade.* to teach. The certificate of [the] second grade shall be granted only to those who shall have taught at least seven months with ability and success, and it shall be valid throughout the county for which it shall be granted for three years. The certificates of the third grade shall be *Third grade.* divided into two classes known as A and B. Third grade *Classes A and B.* certificates of class A shall be granted only to persons who have taught successfully and continuously for at least three years next preceding the examination in primary departments of graded schools; and a certificate of this class shall entitle the holder to teach in primary departments of graded schools only. Third grade certificates of class B shall license the holder to teach in any school of the county in which it shall be granted for one year; but no more than three certificates of this class shall be granted *Proviso.* to the same person: *Provided*, That the county commissioner shall have power, upon personal examination satisfactory to himself or herself, to grant certificates which shall license the holder thereof to teach in a specified district for which it shall be granted; but such certificate shall not continue in force beyond the time of the next public examination, and in no case shall a second special certificate be granted to the same person, and it shall not in any way exempt the teacher from a full examination.

Suspension of certificate, etc. (§132.) SEC. 7. The board of school examiners may suspend or revoke any teachers' certificate issued by them for any reason which would have justified said board in withholding the same when given, for neglect of duty, for incompetency to instruct or govern a school, or for immorality; and the said board may, within their jurisdiction, suspend for immorality or incompetency to instruct and govern a school, the effect of any teachers' certificate that *Proviso.* may have been granted by other lawful authority: *Provided*, That no certificates shall be suspended or revoked without a personal hearing, unless the holder thereof shall, after a reasonable notice, neglect or refuse to appear before the said board for that purpose.

Duty of commissioner. (§133.) SEC. 8. It shall be the duty of the county commissioner:

First, Immediately after his or her qualification as com- Notice of quali-
missioner, to send notice thereof to the Superintendent of cation.
Public Instruction and the chairman of each township
board of school inspectors of the county;

Second, To keep a record of all examinations held by Record of exam-
the board of school examiners and to sign all certificates inations, etc.
and other papers and reports issued by the board;

Third, To receive the institute fees provided by law and Of fees.
to pay the same to the county treasurer quarterly, beginning September thirty, in each year;

Fourth, To keep a record of all certificates granted, sus- Record of cer-
pended, or revoked by the said board or commissioner, tificates.
showing to whom issued, together with the date, grade,
duration of each certficate and, if suspended or revoked,
with the date and reason thereof;

Fifth, To furnish, previous to the first Monday in Sep- List of teachers,
tember in each year to the township clerk of each town- etc.
ship in the county, a list of all persons legally authorized
to teach in the county at large, and in such township,
with the date and term of each certificate, and if any
have been suspended or revoked, the date of such suspension or revocation;

Sixth, To visit each of the schools in the county at To visit schools,
least once in each year and to examine carefully the dis- etc.
cipline, the mode of instruction, and the progress and pro-
ficiency of pupils: *Provided,* That in case the county com- Proviso as to
missioner is unable to visit all the schools of the county assistant visit-
as herein required, the said commissioner may appoint such
assistant visitors as may be necessary, who shall perform
such duties pertaining to the visitation and supervision of
schools as said commissioner shall direct: *Provided,* That
the whole expense incurred by such assistant visitor shall
not exceed the sum of ninety dollars in any one year;

Seventh, To counsel with the teachers and school boards Counsel with
as to the courses of study to be pursued, and as to any teachers, etc.
improvement in the discipline and instruction in the schools;

Eighth, To promote by such means as he or she may Improvement of
devise, the improvement of the schools in the county, and schools, etc.
the elevation of the character and qualifications of the
teachers and officers thereof, and act as assistant conductor
of institutes appointed by the Superintendent of Public
Instruction and perform such other duties pertaining thereto
as the superintendent shall require;

Ninth, To receive the duplicate annual reports of the To receive an-
several boards of school inspectors, examine into the cor- nual reports,
rectness of the same, requiring them to be amended when etc.
necessary, indorse his or her approval upon them, and
immediately thereafter and before the first day of November in each year, transmit to the Superintendent of Public
Instruction one copy of each of said reports and file the
other in the office of the county clerk;

Tenth, To be subject to such instructions and rules as the
Superintendent of Public Instruction may prescribe, to

Subject to instructions of Supt. of Public Instruction, etc. receive all blanks and communications that may be sent to him or her by the Superintendent of Public Instruction and to dispose of the same as directed by the said superintendent, and to make annual reports at the close of the school year to the Superintendent of Public Instruction of his or her official labor, and of the schools of the county, together with such other information as may be required;

Other duties. *Eleventh,* To perform such other duties as may be required of him or her by law, and at the close of the term of office to deliver all records, books, and papers belonging to the office, to his or her successor.

Duty of chairman, etc. (§134.) SEC. 9. It shall be the duty of the chairman of the board of school inspectors of each township:

Supervision of schools, etc. *First,* To have general supervisory charge of the schools of his township, subject to such advice and direction as the county commissioner may give;

To make reports, etc. *Second,* To make such reports of his official labors and of the condition of the schools as the Superintendent of Public Instruction may direct or commissioner request.

Compensation of commissioner. (§135.) SEC. 10. The compensation of each commissioner shall be determined by the board of supervisors of each county respectively, but the compensation shall not be fixed at a sum less than five hundred dollars per annum in any county where there are fifty schools under his or her supervision, at not less than one thousand dollars per annum where there are one hundred schools under such supervision, and not less than twelve hundred dollars where there are one hundred and twenty-five schools under his supervision; and in no case shall such compensation exceed the sum of fifteen hundred dollars per annum. Each member of the board of school examiners other than the county commissioner shall receive four dollars for each day actually employed in the duties of his office. The compensation of any assistant visitor, when appointed as provided in this act, shall be determined by the county commissioner, but in no case shall it exceed three dollars for each day employed. The compensation of the county commissioner, members of the board of school examiners, and of any assistant visitor shall be paid quarterly from the county treasury, upon such commissioner or visitor filing with the county clerk a certified statement of his or her account, which shall give in separate items the nature and amount of the service for each day for which compensation is claimed: *Provided,* That in no case shall the county commissioner receive any order for compensation from the county clerk until he has filed a certified statement from the Superintendent of Public Instruction that all reports required of the commissioner have been properly made and filed with said superintendent: *Provided further,* That no commissioner shall receive an order for compensation until he shall have filed with the county clerk a detailed statement under oath showing what schools have been

Of examiners.

Of assistant visitors.

To be paid quarterly.

Proviso.

Further proviso.

visited by him during the preceding quarter and what amount of time was employed in each school, naming the township and school district. The necessary contingent expenses of the commissioner for printing, postage, stationery, record books, and rent of rooms for public examinations shall be audited and allowed by the board of supervisors of the county; but in no county shall the expenses so allowed exceed the sum of two hundred dollars per annum and no traveling fees shall be allowed to the commissioner or to any assistant visitor or school examiner. *Of contingent expenses. Limit of.*

(§136.) SEC. 11. No Superintendent of Public Instruction, instructor at institute, county commissioner or examiner, shall act as agent for the sale of any school furniture, text books, maps, charts, or other school apparatus. *Shall not act as agent, etc. See ¶ 146.*

(§137.) SEC. 12. Whenever by death, resignation, removal from office, or otherwise a vacancy shall occur in the office of the county commissioner of schools, the county clerk shall issue a call to the chairman of the township board of school inspectors of each township in the county, who shall meet at the office of the county clerk on a date to be named in said [notices] notice, not more than ten days from the date of the notice, and appoint a suitable person to fill the vacancy for the unexpired portion of the term of office. *Of vacancies. See § 126.*

(§138.) SEC. 13. The officers of every school district which is or shall hereafter be organized in whole or in part in any incorporated city in this State where special enactments shall exist in regard to the licensing of teachers, shall employ only such teachers as are legally qualified under the provisions of this act: *Provided,* That in cities employing a superintendent, the examination of teachers shall be conducted by such superintendent or by a committee of the board of education of such school district, and certificate issued at such time and in such a manner as the Superintendent of Public Instruction and board of education in such city shall prescribe. Cities having a special and thoroughly equipped normal training department, under control of a special training teacher, such school having a course of not less than one year, shall be exempt from the provisions of this section as to the examination of teachers. Any board of education that shall violate the provisions of this act by employing a teacher who is not legally qualified, shall forfeit such a proportion of the primary school interest fund as the number of unqualified teachers employed bears to the whole number of teachers employed in the district. All . school districts organized by special enactments, shall, through their proper officers, make such reports as the Superintendent of Public Instruction may require. *Certain schools exempted, etc. Of city schools. Exempt from licensing of teachers, etc.*

§139. SEC. 14. All acts or parts of acts conflicting with the provisions of this act are hereby repealed. *Repealing clause.*

CHAPTER XIII.

PENALTIES AND LIABILITIES.

Penalty on inhabitant for neglect of duty.

(§140.) SECTION 1. Any taxable inhabitant of a newly formed district receiving the notice of the first meeting, who shall neglect or refuse duly to serve and return such notice, and every chairman of the first district meeting in any district, who shall wilfully neglect or refuse to perform the duties enjoined on him by this act shall respectively forfeit the sum of five dollars.

Penalty on district officer for neglecting or refusing to perform duties.
See App. A, ¶¶ 158, 160.

(§141.) SEC. 2. Any person duly elected to the office of moderator, director, assessor, or trustee of a school district, who shall neglect or refuse without sufficient cause, to accept such office and serve therein or who, having entered upon the duties of his office, shall neglect or refuse to perform any duty required of him by virtue of his office, shall forfeit the sum of ten dollars.

Penalty on inspector for neglect or refusal.

(§142.) SEC. 3. Any person duly elected or appointed a school inspector, who shall neglect or refuse, without sufficient cause, to qualify and serve as such, or who, having entered upon the duties of his office, shall neglect or refuse to perform any duty required of him by virtue of his office, shall forfeit the sum of ten dollars.

Liability of inspectors for neglecting to report.
See App. A, ¶¶ 5-11.

(§143.) SEC. 4. If any board of school inspectors shall neglect or refuse to make and deliver to the township clerk their annual report as required by this act, within the time limited therefor, they shall be liable to pay the full amount of money lost by their failure, with interest thereon, to be recovered by the township treasurer in the name of the township, in an action of debt or on the case; and if any township clerk shall neglect or refuse to transmit the report herein mentioned within the time limited therefor, he shall be liable to pay the full amount lost by such neglect or refusal, with interest thereon, to be recovered in an action of debt or on the case.

Liability of township clerk.

Liability of county clerk for neglect to transmit reports.

(§144.) SEC. 5. Any county clerk who shall neglect or refuse to transmit to the Superintendent of Public Instruction the reports required by this act, within the time therefor limited, shall be liable to pay to each township the full amount which such township or any school district therein, shall lose by such neglect or refusal, with interest thereon, to be recovered in an action of debt or on the case.

How moneys collected on account of neglect disposed of.

(§145.) SEC. 6. All the moneys collected or received by any township treasurer under the provisions of either of the two last preceding sections, shall be apportioned and distributed to the school districts entitled thereto, in the same manner and in the same proportion that the moneys lost by any neglect or refusal therein mentioned would, according to the provisions of this act, have been apportioned and distributed.

(§146.) Sec. 7. Any township clerk who shall neglect Liability of township clerk and supervisor in regard to district taxes. or refuse to certify to the supervisor any school district axes that have been reported to him as required by this ict, and any supervisor wilfully neglecting to assess any such tax shall be liable to any district for any damage occasioned thereby, to be recovered by the assessor in the name of the district, in an action of debt or on the case.

(§147.) Sec. 8. The township board of each township, When township board to remove certain officers. and in the case of fractional school districts, the township board of the township in which the district schoolhouse thereof is situated, shall have power and is hereby required to remove from office, upon satisfactory proof, after at least See App. A, ¶¶ 12, 17. five days' notice to the party implicated, any district officer or school inspector who shall have illegally used or disposed of any of the public moneys entrusted to his charge, or who shall persistently and without sufficient cause, refuse or neglect to discharge any of the duties of his office. And in case of such removal it shall be the Township clerk to record order for removal. duty of the township clerk of such township to enter in the records of such township the resolution or order of such board, for such removal; and such record of such resolution or order so entered, or a certified copy thereof, shall be *prima facie* evidence in all courts and places of the jurisdiction of such board and of the regularity of the proceedings for such removal, and (unless the party Party removed may institute proceedings for removal of order of township board. so removed shall, within thirty days after such removal, institute proceedings before a court of competent jurisdiction for the removal of such order for removal, or if after such thirty days such proceedings to obtain such removal shall be discontinued or dismissed) shall be conclusive evidence of jurisdiction and regularity, if it shall appear that the party so removed had five days' notice of the time and place fixed by said board for the hearing of the case as aforesaid.

(§148.) Sec. 9. No school officer, superintendent, or School officers and teachers not to act as school-book agents, etc. teacher of schools, shall act as agent for any author, publisher, or seller of school books, or shall directly or indirectly receive any gift or reward for his influence in School officers not to be interested in contracts in certain cases. recommending the purchase or use of any library or school book or school apparatus, or furniture whatever, nor shall any school officer be personally interested in any way whatever in any contract with the district in which he may hold office. Any act or neglect herein prohibited, Such acts deemed misdemeanors. performed by any such officer, superintendent, or teacher, shall be deemed a misdemeanor.

(§149.) Sec. 10. All provisions of this act shall apply Where this act shall apply. and be in force in every school district, township, city, and village in this State, except such as may be inconsistent with the direct provisions of some special enactment of the Legislature.

(§150.) Sec. 11. Chapters numbered one hundred thirty- Chapters and acts repealed. one, one hundred thirty-six, one hundred thirty-seven, and

8

one hundred thirty-eight of the compiled laws of eighteen hundred seventy-one, and act numbered forty-two of the session laws of eighteen hundred seventy-five, and all acts and parts of acts amendatory of said chapters and said act, being acts numbered forty-one, forty-two, fifty-six, and sixty-three of the session laws of eighteen hundred seventy-two; acts numbered forty-four, sixty-nine, seventy-one, seventy-six, ninety-eight, one hundred nineteen, one hundred thirty-two, one hundred sixty-four, and one hundred ninety-three of the session laws of eighteen hundred seventy-three; acts numbered thirty-six, fifty-one, eighty-four, ninety-four, one hundred six, one hundred thirty-seven, one hundred eighty-three, and two hundred thirty of the session laws of eighteen hundred seventy-five; acts numbered seventy-seven and one hundred seventy-three of the session laws of eighteen hundred seventy-seven; acts numbered forty-four, forty-six, one hundred fifty-nine, one hundred sixty-four, two hundred fifty-four, two hundred fifty-five, and two hundred sixty-four of the session laws of eighteen hundred seventy-nine; and all other acts and parts of acts contravening the provisions of this act are hereby fully repealed.

CHAPTER XIV.

[Act No. 158, Laws of 1881.]

ELECTION OF SCHOOL INSPECTORS.

Sections amended. (§151.) SECTION 1. Sections eight and fourteen of chapter twelve of the compiled laws of eighteen hundred and seventy-one, as amended by act number forty-two of the session laws of eighteen hundred seventy-five, are hereby amended; and section thirteen of the same chapter, repealed by said act, is hereby restored and amended; and section one hundred and three of the same chapter, as amended by act number one hundred ninety-nine of the session laws of eighteen hundred seventy-nine, is hereby amended, all of said sections to read as follows:

Annual meeting. (§152.) SEC. 2. The annual meeting of each township shall be held on the first Monday in April in each year, and at such meeting there shall be an election for the **Officers to be elected.** following officers: one supervisor, one township clerk, one treasurer, one school inspector, one commissioner of highways, so many justices of the peace as there are by law to be elected in the township, and so many constables as shall be ordered by the meeting, not exceeding four in number.

Term of office of school inspectors. (§153.) SEC. 3. Each school inspector elected as aforesaid shall hold his office for two years from that time and until his successor shall be elected and duly qualified, **Vacancy.** except when elected or appointed to fill a vacancy, in which case he shall hold the office during the unexpired

portion of the regular term: *Provided*, That in the year _{Proviso.}
eighteen hundred eighty-two one additional school inspector
in each township shall be elected for the term of one
year: *Provided further*, That the township superintendent _{Proviso.}
of schools and school inspectors now in office shall
continue to act as school inspectors, and said superintendent of schools shall continue to act as chairman of
the board of school inspectors until the school inspectors
provided for by this act shall have been elected and duly
qualified and shall enter upon the duties of their respective offices.

(§154.) SEC. 4. Each of the officers elected at such _{Term of office.}
meetings, except justices of the peace and school inspect-
ors, shall hold his office for the term of one year and
until his successor shall be elected and duly qualified.

(§155.) SEC. 5. No person, except an elector as afore- _{Who eligible to office.}
said, shall be eligible to any elective office contemplated
in this chapter: *Provided, however*, That any female per- _{Proviso.}
son of or above the age of twenty-one years, who has
resided in this State three months and in the township
ten days next preceding any election, shall be eligible to
the office of school inspector.

CHAPTER XV.

[Act No. 53, Laws of 1877.]

TEACHERS' INSTITUTES.

(§156.) SECTION 1. All boards or officers authorized by _{Examining officers to collect fees from teachers.}
law to examine applicants for certificates of qualification
as teachers shall collect, at the time of examination from
each male applicant for a certificate, an annual fee of one
dollar, and from each female applicant for a certificate, an
annual fee of fifty cents; and the director or secretary of
any school board that shall employ any teacher who has
not paid the fee hereinbefore provided, shall collect at the
time of making contract, from each male teacher so
employed, an annual fee of one dollar, and from each
female teacher so employed, an annual fee of fifty cents.
All persons paying a fee, as required by this section, shall
be given a receipt for the same, and no person shall be
required to pay said fee more than once, in any school
year.

(§157.) SEC. 2. All such fees collected by the director _{Fees to be paid to county treasurer quarterly.}
or secretary of any school board shall be paid over to
the secretary of the county board of school examiners of
the county in which they were collected, on or before the
fifteenth day of March, June, September and December,

(§156.) The requirements of the statutes apply to all teachers, whether applicants for
certificates, or employed by school boards, save that but one fee can be required for any
one year.—*Van Riper, Attorney General, March 21, 1894.*

accompanied by a list of those persons from whom they were collected; and all of such fees, together with all those that shall be collected by the county board of school examiners, shall be paid over by the secretary of said board of school examiners to the treasurer of the county in which they were collected, on or before the last day of March, June, September, and December, in each year, accompanied by a complete list of all persons from whom said fees were collected; and a like list, accompanied by a statement from the county treasurer that said fees have been paid to him, shall be sent by said secretary to the Superintendent **Fees so paid to constitute teachers' institute fund.** of Public Instruction. All moneys paid over to the county treasurer as provided by this act, shall be set apart as a teachers' institute fund, to be used as hereinafter provided.

(§158.) SEC. 3. The Superintendent of Public Instruc- **Annual county institute.** tion shall annually appoint a time and place in each organized county for holding a teachers' institute, make suitable **Proviso.** arrangements therefor, and give due notice thereof: *Provided,* That in organized counties having less than one thousand children between the ages of five and twenty years, the holding of said institute shall be optional with the said superintendent, unless requested to hold such institute by fifteen teachers of the county in which such **Proviso.** institute is to be held: *Provided, however,* That if there shall not be a sufficient number of teachers in any county to make such request, then teachers of adjoining counties who desire to attend such institute may unite in the **Proviso.** required application to said superintendent: *Provided also,* That the said superintendent may, in his discretion, hold an institute for the benefit of two or more adjoining counties and draw the institute fund from each of the counties thus benefited, as hereinafter provided.

Conductor of institute may be appointed. (§159.) SEC. 4. The Superintendent of Public Instruction, in case of inability personally to conduct any institute or to make the necessary arrangements for holding the same, is hereby authorized to appoint some suitable person for that purpose, who shall be subject to the direction of said superintendent. Every teacher attending any institute held in accordance with the provisions of this act, shall be given by the Superintendent of Public Instruction or by the duly appointed conductor, a certificate setting forth at what sessions of said institute such **Teachers can close school to attend institute.** teacher shall have been in attendance; and any teacher who shall have closed his or her school in order to attend said institute shall not forfeit his or her wages as teacher during such time as he or she shall have been in attendance at said institute, and the certificate hereinbefore provided shall be evidence of such attendance.

Expenses of institute, how paid. (§160.) SEC. 5. For the purpose of defraying the expenses of rooms, fires, lights, or other necessary charges, and for procuring teachers and lecturers, the said superintendent or the person duly authorized by him to conduct said institute, may demand [an order] of the county clerk of each county for the benefit of which the institute is held, who shall thereupon draw an order on the county treasurer of his county for such sum, not exceeding the amount of the institute fund in the county treasury, as may be necessary to defray the expenses of said institute; and the treasurer of said county is hereby required to pay over to said superintendent or duly appointed institute conductor, from the institute funds in his hands, the amount of said order.

(§161.) SEC. 6 In case the institute fund in any county shall be insufficient to defray the necessary expenses of any institute held under the provisions of this act, the Auditor General shall, upon the certificate of the superintendent that he has made arrangements for holding such institute and that the county institute fund is insufficient to meet the expenses thereof, draw his warrant upon the State Treasurer for such additional sum as said superintendent shall deem necessary for conducting such institute, which sum shall not exceed sixty dollars for each institute of five days' duration, and shall be paid out of the general fund. *May draw on State treasurer, in certain cases.*

(§162.) SEC. 7. The Superintendent is authorized to hold, once in each year, an institute for the State at large to be denominated a State institute; and for the purpose of defraying the necessary expenses of such institute, the Auditor General shall, on the certificate of said superintendent that he has made arrangements for holding such institute, draw his warrant upon the State Treasurer for such sum as said superintendent shall deem necessary for conducting such institute, which sum shall not exceed four hundred dollars and shall be paid out of the general fund: *Provided*, That not more than eighteen hundred dollars shall be drawn from the treasury, or any greater liability incurred in any one year, to meet the provisions of this act. *Yearly State institute. Expenses to be paid from State treasury. Proviso.*

(§163.) SEC. 8. The Superintendent of Public Instruction, or the conductor of the institute by him appointed, drawing money from the county treasurer under section five of this act, shall, at the close of each institute, furnish to the county treasurer vouchers for all payments from the same in accordance with this act; and he shall return to the county treasurer whatever of the amount that may remain unexpended, to be replaced in the institute fund. *Vouchers for payments.*

(§164.) SEC. 9. An act entitled "An Act to establish Teachers' Institutes," approved February tenth, eighteen hundred ‑fifty-five, as amended by act two hundred thirty-nine, session laws of eighteen hundred sixty-one, being compiler's sections three thousand seven hundred eighty-nine, three thousand seven hundred ninety, and three thousand seven hundred ninety-one of the compiled laws of eighteen hundred seventy-one, are hereby repealed. *Acts repealed.*

CHAPTER XVI.

[From Act No. 194, Laws of 1889.]

NORMAL SCHOOL DIPLOMAS AND CERTIFICATES.

Of the Normal School. (§165.) SEC. 3. The State Board of Education shall continue the normal school at Ypsilanti in the county of Washtenaw, where it is now located. The purpose of the normal school shall be the instruction of persons in the art of teaching, and in all the various branches pertain- **Proviso.** ing to the public schools of the State of Michigan: *Provided*, There shall be prescribed for said school a course of study intended specially to prepare students for the rural and the elementary [graded] schools of this State, which shall provide not less than twenty weeks of special professional instruction.

Course of study, training school, etc. (§166.) SEC. 5. Said board shall provide all necessary courses of study to be pursued in the normal school, and establish and maintain in connection therewith a fully equipped training school as a school of observation and practice, and shall grant, upon the completion of either of said courses, such diplomas as it may deem best; and **Diplomas.** such diploma, when granted, shall carry with it such honors as the extent of the course for which the diploma is given may warrant and said Board of Education may direct.

Certificate to teach, when granted, term of, etc. (§167.) SEC. 6. Upon the completion of the course specially prescribed, as hereinbefore provided for the rural and elementary graded schools, said Board of Education shall, upon the recommendation of the principal and a majority **See App. A, 92, §§ 130, 169, 233.** of the heads of departments of said school, grant a certificate which shall be signed by said board and the principal of the normal school, which certificate shall contain a list of the studies included in said course and which shall entitle the holder to teach in any of the schools of the State for which said course has been provided for a **Proviso.** period of five years: *Provided*, That said certificate may be suspended or revoked by said State Board of Education upon cause shown by any county board of examination, or by any board of school officers.

Life certificates, when granted, etc. (§168.) SEO 7. Upon the completion of either of the advanced courses of study prescribed by said State board, which shall require not less than four years for their completion, said Board of Education, upon the recommendation of the principal and a majority of the heads of departments of said school, shall issue a certificate to the person completing said course, which certificate shall be referred to in the diploma hereinbefore provided to be **May be revoked.** granted. Said certificate shall set forth a list of the studies of the course completed and, when given, shall

)perate as a ·life certificate, unless revoked by said State
Board of Education.

(§169.) SEC. 8. The Board of Education shall make such Admission of
regulations for the admission of pupils to said school as it pupils.
;hall deem necessary and proper: *Provided,* That the appli- Proviso.
cant shall, before admission, sign a declaration of intention
to teach in the schools in this State.

CHAPTER XVII.

[From Act No. 73, Laws of 1895.]

STATE CERTIFICATES TO TEACHERS.

(§170.) SEC. 15. Said board shall hold at least two meet- Board to grant
ings each year, at which they shall examine teachers and certificates, etc.
shall grant certificates to such as have taught in the
schools of this State at least two years, and who shall,
upon a thorough and critical examination in every study
required for such certificate, be found to possess eminent
scholarship, ability and good moral character. Such certificate shall be signed by the members of said board and
be impressed with its seal, and shall entitle holder to
teach in any of the public schools of this State without
further examination, and shall be valid for life, unless
revoked by said board. No certificate shall be granted
except upon the examination herein prescribed: *Provided,*
That the said State Board of Education may, in its dis- Certificates of
cretion, endorse State teachers' certificates or normal school other states.
diplomas granted in other States, if it be shown to the
satisfaction of such board that the examinations required
or courses of study pursued are fully equal to the requirements of this State.

CHAPTER XVIII.

[Act No. 117, Laws of 1855.]

TEACHERS' ASSOCIATIONS.

(§171.) SECTION 1. Any fifteen or more teachers, or Fifteen or more
other persons residing in this State, who shall associate teachers may
for the purpose of promoting education and science, and tion.
improvements in the theory and practice of teaching, may
form themselves into a corporation, under such name as
they may choose, providing they shall have published in Notice to be
some newspaper printed at Lansing or in the county in published.
which such association is to be located, for at least one
month previous, a notice of the time, place, and purpose
of the meeting for such association, and shall file in the Constitution,
where filed,

office of the Secretary of State a copy of the constitution and by-laws of said association.

May hold property. (§172.) SEC. 2. Such association may hold and possess real and personal property to the amount of five thousand dollars; but the funds or property thereof shall not be used for any other purpose than the legitimate business of the association in securing the objects of its corporation.

Restrictions upon its use.

Privileges and liabilities of corporations. (§173.) SEC. 3. Upon becoming a corporation as hereinbefore provided, they shall have all the powers and privileges, and be subject to all the duties of a corporation, according to the provisions of chapter fifty-five of the revised statutes of this State [Chap. 130, compiled laws of 1871], so far as such provisions shall be applicable in such case and not inconsistent with the provisions of this act.

CHAPTER XIX.

[Act No. 131, Laws of 1875.]

SAFE KEEPING OF PUBLIC MONEYS.

"Public moneys" defined.

See App. A, ¶¶ 50-79. (§174.) SECTION 1. All moneys which shall come into the hands of any officer of the State, or of any officer of any county, or of any township, school district, highway district, city, or village, or of any other municipal or public corporation within this State, pursuant to any provision of law authorizing such officer to receive the same, shall be denominated public moneys within the meaning of this act.

Public moneys to be kept separate from all other funds. (§175.) SEC. 2. It shall be the duty of every officer charged with the receiving, keeping or disbursing of public moneys to keep the same separate and apart from his own money, and he shall not commingle the same with his own money, nor with the money of any other person, firm, or corporation.

How used. (§176.) SEC. 3. No such officer shall, under any pretext, use nor allow to be used, any such moneys for any purpose other than in accordance with the provisions of law; nor shall he use the same for his own private use, nor loan the same to any person, firm, or corporation, without legal authority so to do.

Interest on public moneys to constitute a general fund. (§177.) SEC. 4. In all cases where public moneys are authorized to be deposited in any bank, or to be loaned to any individual, firm, or corporation, for interest, the interest accruing upon such public moneys shall belong to and constitute a general fund of the State, county, or other public or municipal corporation, as the case may be.

Officers not to receive consideration for deposit of money with particular bank, etc. (§178.) SEC. 5. In no case shall any such officer, directly or indirectly, receive any pecuniary or valuable consideration as an inducement for the deposit of any public moneys with any particular bank, person, firm, or corporation.

(§179.) SEC. 6. The provisions of this act shall apply to all deputies of such officer or officers, and to all clerks, agents, and servants of such officer or officers. Provisions of this act to apply to deputies, etc.

(§180.) SEC. 7. Any person guilty of a violation of any of the provisions of this act shall, on conviction thereof, be punished by a fine not exceeding one thousand dollars, or imprisonment in the county jail not exceeding six months, or both such fine and imprisonment in the discretion of the court: *Provided*, That nothing in this act contained shall prevent a prosecution under the general statute for embezzlement in cases where the facts warrant a prosecution under such general statute. Penalty for violating provisions of this act. Proviso.

(§181.) SEC. 8. Any officer who shall wilfully or corruptly draw or issue any warrant, order, or certificate for the payment of money in excess of the amount authorized by law, or for a purpose not authorized by law, shall be deemed guilty of a misdemeanor, and may be punished as provided in the preceding section. Penalty for illegal payment of money.

CHAPTER XX.

[Act No. 95, Public Acts of 1895.]

COMPULSORY EDUCATION OF CHILDREN.

(§182.) SECTION. 1. *The People of the State of Michigan enact*, That every parent guardian or other person in the State of Michigan having control and charge of any child or children between the ages of eight and fourteen years, and in cities between the ages of seven and sixteen years, shall be required to send such child or children to the public school for a period of at least four months in each school year, except that, in cities having a duly constituted police force, the attendance at school shall not be limited to four months, beginning on the first Monday of the first term commencing in his or her district after September 1, 1895, and of each year thereafter. Such attendance shall be consecutive and each and every pupil between the ages specified shall have attended school the entire four months previous to the thirtieth day of June in each school year: *Provided*, If it be shown that such child or children are being taught in a private school in such branches as are usually taught in the public schools, or have already acquired the ordinary branches of learning taught in public schools, or if the person or persons in parental relation to such child or children present a written statement that such child or children are physically unable to attend school, the truant officer or district board may employ a reputable physician to examine such child or children; and if such physician shall certify that such child or children are physically unable to attend school, Duty of parents and guardians to send children to school. Proviso.

9

such child or children shall be exempt from the provisions of this act: *And further provided*, In case a public school shall not be taught for four months during the time specified, within two miles by the nearest traveled road of the residence of any person within the school district, he or she shall not be liable to the provisions of this act.

Truant officer. (§183.) SEC. 2. The district board or board of education in each school district in the State which has been organized as a graded school district or as a township district according to the laws of the State, shall, at its first meeting, after this law goes into effect and previous to the tenth day of September of each year, appoint a truant officer for the term of one year from and after the first Monday of September of each year. In townships whose districts have been organized under the primary school law, the chairman of the township board of school inspectors shall be the truant officer and shall perform all the duties of truant officer, as provided for in this act, so far as the provisions of this law applies to the territory over which he has **In cities.** jurisdiction: *Provided*, That in cities having a duly organized police force, it shall be the duty of the police authorities, at the request of the school authorities, to detail one or more members of said force to perform the duties of **Compensation of truant officer.** truant officer. The compensation of the truant officer shall be fixed in graded school districts by the board which appoints, and in townships by the township board, and in no case shall such compensation be less than one dollar and fifty cents per day for time actually employed under the direction of the school board in performance of his official duties. The compensation of truant officers shall be allowed and paid in the same manner as incidental expenses are paid by such boards.

Duty of truant officer. (§184.) SEC. 3. It shall be the duty of the truant officer to investigate all cases of truancy or non-attendance at school, and render all service within his power to compel children to attend school; and, when informed of continued non-attendance by any teacher or resident of the school district, he shall immediately notify the persons having control of such children that, on the following Monday, such children shall present themselves with the necessary text books for instruction in the proper school or schools of **Notice to parents.** the district. The notice shall inform said parent or guardian that attendance at school must be consecutive at least eight half days of each week, until the end of that term; except in cities having a duly constituted police **Penalty.** force, attendance in school shall be continuous. In case any parent, guardian, or other person shall fail to comply with the provisions of this act, he shall be deemed guilty of a misdemeanor and shall, on conviction, be liable to a fine of not less than five dollars nor more than fifty dollars, or by imprisonment in the county or city jail for not less than two nor more than ninety days, or by both such fine and imprisonment in the discretion of the court.

(§185.) SEC. 4. In all city school districts in this State having a school census of five hundred or more pupils, the school board or officers having in charge the schools of such districts may establish one or more ungraded schools for the instruction of certain children, as defined and set forth in the following section. They may, through their truant officer and superintendent of schools, require such children to attend said ungraded schools, or any department of their graded schools, as said board of education may direct. *Ungraded school.*

(§186.) SEC. 5. The following classes of persons between the ages of eight and fourteen years, and in cities between the ages of seven and sixteen years, shall be deemed juvenile disorderly persons and shall, in the judgment of the proper school authorities, be assigned to the ungraded school or schools as provided in section four of this act: class one, habitual truants from any school in which they are enrolled as pupils; class two, children who, while attending any school, are incorrigibly turbulent, disobedient, or insubordinate, or are vicious or immoral in conduct; class three, children who are not attending any school and who habitually frequent streets and other public places, having no lawful business, employment, or occupation. *Juvenile disorderly persons.*

(§187.) SEC. 6. It shall be the duty of the truant officer, in case of a violation of this law, within one week after having given the notice to the parent or guardian as specified in section three, to make a complaint against said parent, guardian, or other person having the legal charge and control of such child, before a justice of the peace in the city, village, or township where the party resides, (except in cities having recorder's or police court) for such refusal or neglect; and said justice of the peace, police judge, or recorder's court shall issue a warrant upon said complaint and shall proceed to hear and determine the same; and upon conviction thereof said parent, guardian or other person as the case may be, shall be punished according to provisions of section three of this act. It shall be the duty of all school officers, superintendents, or teachers, to render such assistance and furnish such information as they have at their command, to aid said truant officer in the fulfillment of his official duties. *Further duty of truant officer.* *Complaint and warrant.*

(§188.) SEC. 7. When, in the judgment of school boards of primary and township school districts or the superintendent of city schools and the truant officer, it becomes certain that all legal means have been exhausted in their attempts to compel the attendance at school of a juvenile disorderly person, the truant officer shall, in case the person in parental relation to the child neglects or refuses to do so, make a complaint against such juvenile disorderly person before a court of competent jurisdiction, that said *Commitment to reformatory.*

child is a juvenile disorderly person as described in section
five of this act. The justice of the peace or court shall
issue a warrant and proceed to hear such complaint; and, if
said justice of the peace or court shall determine that said
child is a juvenile disorderly person within the meaning of
this act, then said justice of the peace or court shall thereupon and after consultation with the county agent of cor-
rections and charities, sentence such child, if a boy, to the
Industrial School for Boys at Lansing for a term not extending beyond the time when said child shall arrive at the age
of seventeen years, unless sooner discharged by the board
of control of said Industrial School for Boys; or, if a girl,
to the Industrial Home for Girls at Adrian, for a term
not extending beyond the time when said child shall
arrive at the age of seventeen years, unless sooner discharged by the board of control of said Industrial Home
for Girls: *Provided, however*, That such sentence shall, in
case of the first offense, be suspended.

(§189.) Sec. 8. All acts or parts of acts conflicting
with the provisions of this act are hereby repealed.

CHAPER XXIII.

[Act No. 222, Public Acts of 1837.]

TO PREVENT CRIME AND PUNISH TRUANCY.

Certain girls
and boys deemed
truant and dis-
orderly persons.

(§190.) SECTION 1. *The People of the State of Michigan
enact,* That every boy between the ages of ten and sixteen
years or any girl between the ages of ten and seventeen
years, who shall frequent or be found lounging about
saloons or other rooms or places where intoxicating liquors
are kept for sale, or who shall, against the command of
his or her parent or guardian, run away or wilfully absent
himself or herself from the school he or she is attending,
or from any house, office, shop, farm or other place where
he or she is residing or legitimately employed to labor,
or shall, against such command of his or her parent or
guardian, or for an immoral, disorderly, or dishonest purpose, be found lounging upon any public street, highway.
or other public place, or shall, against such command, or
for any such purpose, attend any public dance, skating
rink, or show, shall be deemed to be a truant or disorderly person.

Who to make
complaint.

(§206.) Sec. 2. Upon complaint upon oath and in
writing made before any justice of the peace by the
parent or guardian of any girl between the ages of ten
and seventeen years, or of any boy between ten and sixteen years of age, or by the supervisor of any township,
or the mayor of any city, or president of any village, and
in cities of over eight thousand population, by the chief
of police, that any such minor has been guilty of any of

the acts specified in section one of this act, such justice shall issue his warrant for the arrest of such minor, and upon such conviction, such minor, if a boy, may be sen- Upon conviction, tenced by such justice to the Industrial School for Boys, at where to be sentenced. Lansing; and, if a girl, to the State Industrial Home for Term of Girls at Adrian; boys until seventeen years of age and sentence. girls until twenty-one years of age, unless sooner discharged according to law: *Provided*, That no person or persons Proviso as to shall be sent to said Industrial School for Boys, or the approval of sentence. Industrial Home for Girls, until the sentence therein has been submitted to and approved by the circuit judge of the circuit or the judge of probate of the county in which such conviction shall be had.

(§191.) SEC. 3. The same proceedings shall be had upon Proceedings the trial of any person charged with being guilty of any upon trial. of the offenses mentioned in section one of this act before the justice before whom such person is brought as are had in trials for misdemeanor, as far as the same are applicable; and the State agent for the care of juvenile Duty of State offenders of the county wherein such offenders may be on agent. trial shall have authority and take the same action in the premises as is provided by act number one hundred seventy-one of the session laws of eighteen hundred seventy-three of this State.

CHAPTER XXIV.

[Act No. 147, Public Acts of 1889.]

FREE TEXT-BOOKS.

(§192.) SECTION 1. From and after June thirtieth, eight- District to vote een hundred and ninety, each school board of the State on question of furnishing free shall purchase, when authorized as hereinafter provided, text-books. the text-books used by the pupils of the schools in its See App. A, district in each of the following subjects, to wit: orthogra- ¶ 161. phy, spelling, writing, reading, geography, arithmetic, grammar (including language lessons) national and State history, civil government, and physiology and hygiene; but text books once adopted under the provisions of this act shall not be changed within five years: *Provided*, That the Proviso. text-book on the subject of physiology and hygiene must be approved by the State Board of Education and shall in every way comply with section fifteen of act number one hundred sixty-five of the public acts of eighteen hundred eighty-seven, approved June ninth, eighteen hundred eighty-seven: *And provided further*, That all text-books Proviso. used in any district shall be uniform in any one subject.

(§193.) SEC. 2. The district board of each school dis- District board to trict shall select the kind of text-books on subjects select text-books enumerated in section one, to be taught in schools of their respective districts: *Provided*, That nothing herein contained shall require any change in text-books now in

Vote to be taken at first annual meeting after the passage of this act.

use in such district. They shall cause to be posted in a conspicuous place, at least ten days prior to the first annual school meeting from and after the passage of this act, a notice that those qualified to vote upon the question of raising money in said district shall vote at such annual meeting to authorize said district board to purchase and provide free text-books for the use of the pupils in said district. If a majority of all the voters, as above provided, present at such meeting, shall authorize said board to raise by tax a sum sufficient to comply with the provisions of this act; the district board shall thereupon make a list of such books and file one copy with the township clerk and keep one copy posted in the school, and due notice of such action by the district shall be noted in the annual report of the Superintendent of

District board to purchase text-books when authorized.

Public Instruction. The district board shall take the necessary steps to purchase such books for the use of all pupils in the several schools of their districts, as hereinafter provided. The text-books so purchased shall be the property of the district purchasing the same, and shall be loaned to pupils free of charge, under such rules and regulations for their careful use and return as said district board may

Proviso.

establish: *Provided,* That nothing herein contained shall prevent any person from buying his or her books from the district board of the school in which he or she may

Proviso.

attend: *Provided further,* That nothing herein contained shall prevent any district having once adopted or rejected free text-books, from taking further action on the same at any subsequent annual meeting.

Board to contract with publishers, etc.

(§193.) SEC. 3. It shall be the duty of the district board of any school district adopting free text-books provided for in this act to make a contract with some dealer or publisher to furnish books used in said district at a price not greater than the net wholesale price of such

Proviso.

books: *Provided,* That any district may, if it so desires, authorize its district board to advertise for proposals before making such contract.

Board to make annual estimate of amount to be raised.

(§194.) SEC. 4. The district board of every school district in the State adopting free text-books under this act shall make and prepare annually an estimate of the amount of money necessary to be raised to comply with the conditions of this act, and shall add such amount to the annual estimates made for money to be raised for school purposes for the next ensuing year. Said sum shall be in addition to the amount now provided by law to be raised, which amount each township clerk shall certify to the supervisor of his township to be assessed upon the taxable property of the respective districts as provided by law for raising the regular annual estimates of the respective district boards for school purposes, and when collected shall be paid to the district treasurer in the same manner as all other money belonging to said district is paid

(§195.) SEC. 5. On the first day of February next after *When director to purchase books, etc.* the tax shall have been levied, the director of said district may proceed to purchase the books required by the pupils of his district from the list mentioned in section one of this act, and shall draw his warrant, countersigned by the moderator, upon the treasurer or assessor of the district for the price of the books so purchased, including the cost of transportation.

(§196.) SEC. 6. If the officers of any school district, *Refusal or neglect of duty a misdemeanor.* which has so voted to supply itself with text-books, shall refuse or neglect to purchase at the expense of the district, for the use of the pupils thereof, the text-books as enumerated in section one of this act, or to provide the money therefor as herein prescribed, each officer or member of such board so refusing, or neglecting, shall be deemed guilty of a misdemeanor, and upon conviction *Penalty* thereof before a court of competent jurisdiction, shall be liable to a penalty of not more than fifty dollars or imprisonment in the county jail for a period not exceeding thirty days, or by both such fine and imprisonment in the discretion of the court: *Provided.* That any dis- *Proviso.* trict board may buy its books of local dealers, if the same can be purchased and delivered to the director as cheaply as if bought of the party who makes the lowest bid to the district board: *Provided further,* That school *Further proviso.* districts in cities organized under special charters shall be *In cities boards may submit question to voters of district.* exempt from the provisions of this act; but such districts may, when so authorized by a majority vote of their district boards, submit the question of free text-books to the qualified voters of said districts. If a majority of the qualified electors vote in favor of furnishing free text books, such district boards shall have authority to proceed under the provisions of this act.

CHAPTER XXV.

[Act No. 176, Public Acts of 1891.]

ORGANIZATION OF TOWNSHIP DISTRICTS.

(§197.) SECTION 1. Whenever the qualified electors of *Petition for organization.* any organized township in the upper peninsula desire to become organized into a single school district, they may petition the township board to give notice that, at the succeeding township meeting, the officers for such organized school district will be chosen, and such other business transacted as shall be necessary thereto. Such petition shall be signed by a majority of the qualified electors of the township and shall be filed in the office of the township clerk at least fifteen days prior to the annual township meeting. Upon the receipt and filing of said petition, *Clerk to notify board, etc.* the township clerk shall notify the members of the town-

ship board and the school [inspector] inspectors of the
township to attend a special meeting to be held not more
than five days thereafter, and at which meeting it shall
be the duty of such township board to compare the names
signed to the petition with the names appearing on the
list of registered voters qualified to vote at the preceding
election; and if it be found that a majority of the voters
qualified to vote at the preceding election have signed the
petition that the organized township of which they are
resident be organized as a single school district, they shall
give notice that, at the then succeeding township meeting,
officers will be chosen for such organized school district;
and shall make and file, both with the county clerk and
the secretary* of the board of school inspectors of the
county in which such township is located, a certified copy
of the above mentioned petition, together with their find-

To be single
districts, etc.

ings and doings thereon; and thereupon such township shall
become a single school district which shall be subject to
all the general laws of the State, so far as the same may
be applicable, and said district shall have all the powers
and privileges conferred upon union school districts by
the laws of this State, all the general provisions of which
relating to common or primary schools shall apply and be
enforced in said district, except such as shall be inconsistent with the provisions of this act; and all schools
organized in said district in pursuance of this act, under
the directions and regulations of said board of education,
shall be public and free to all persons actual residents
within the limits thereof, between the ages of five and
twenty years, inclusive, and to such other persons as the

Proviso.

board of education shall admit: *Provided*, That whenever
the majority of electors in any surveyed township in such
organized township shall petition the board of education to
establish a school or schools therein, the said board of
education are hereby authorized and directed within three
months thereafter to organize such school or schools
therein.

Officers of
district.

(§198.) SEC. 2. The officers of said district shall consist
of two trustees, who, together with the clerk and school
inspectors of said township, shall constitute the board of
education of said district. Said trustees shall be elected
by ballot at the annual township meeting of the township,
upon the same ticket and canvassed in the same manner
as township officers required by law to be elected by

Proviso.

ballot: *Provided*, That, at the annual election to be held
in said township next subsequent to the filing of the
petition as set forth in section one of this act, there shall
be elected two trustees for said district by the electors
thereof, one of whom shall hold his office for the term
of one year, and the other one for the term of two years,
and until their successors shall be elected and qualified,

* Commissioner of schools.

and the time for which the person voted for is intended
shall be designated on the ballot; and at each election
thereafter to be held one trustee shall be elected in said
district, who shall hold his office for the term of two
years and until his successor shall be elected and qualified, said trustee to be designated on the ticket or ballot
for "Member of Board of Education."

(§199.) Sec. 3. Within five days after the annual elec- Duty of town-
tion the township clerk shall notify in writing, the persons ship clerk, etc.
elected trustees under this act of their election, and within
five days thereafter said trustees so elected shall take and
subscribe the oath of office prescribed by the constitution
of this State, before any officer authorized to administer
oaths, and file the same with the township clerk. The
term of office of the trustees of said district shall commence on the second Monday following the annual township election at which they are elected.

(§200.) Sec. 4. The members of the board of education Organization of
shall meet on the third Monday of April of each year, at board, etc.
the office of the township clerk, and organize. The school
inspector of the township whose term of office will soonest
expire shall be president of the board and shall be entitled
to vote in all cases. In the absence of the president at
any meeting a majority of the members present may choose
one of their own number president *pro tem*. The township Clerk.
clerk of said township shall be *ex officio* clerk of said board Treasurer.
of education, and shall be entitled to vote thereon; and in
case of the absence of said clerk the board may choose
some suitable person to perform his duties. Said board
shall, on the said third Monday of April in each year,
elect from their own number a treasurer, who shall hold
his office for one year and until his successor is elected
and qualified and may at any time fill a vacancy in the
office of treasurer: *Provided*, That the person appointed Proviso.
to fill a vacancy in the office of treasurer shall hold the
office for the unexpired portion of the term only. The
treasurer of said board shall, within five days after his
appointment as such treasurer, file with the clerk of said
board the constitutional oath of office. He shall also, To give bond.
before entering upon the duties of his office, give a bond
to said district in such sum and with such sureties as
said board shall determine and approve, conditioned for
the faithful performance of his duties under this act, and
honestly accounting for all moneys coming into his hands
belonging to said district. The treasurer of said board
shall have the keeping of all school and library moneys,
and shall not pay out the same without the authority of
the board, upon warrants or orders drawn upon him and
signed by the clerk and countersigned by the president.

(§201.) Sec. 5. Said board of education shall have power Vacancies.
to fill vacancies that may occur in the office of trustee
until the next annual election, and such trustee shall file

10

with the clerk of said board his oath of office within five days after such appointment by the board.

Quorum, meetings, etc.

(§202.) SEC. 6. A majority of the members of said board shall constitute a quorum, and the regular meetings of said board shall be held on the third Monday of April, August, and December in each year, and no notice of such meeting shall be required; and any two members of said board shall be' sufficient to adjourn any meeting from time to time, until a quorum is present. Special meetings of said board may be called at any time on the request of the president or any two members thereof, in writing, delivered to the clerk, and the clerk upon receiving such request shall at once notify each member of said board, if within said district, of the time of holding such meeting, which shall be at least three days subsequent to the time of receiving such request by said clerk. All [the] meetings of said board shall be held at the township clerk's office, unless otherwise ordered by a resolution of the board; and all records and papers of said district shall be kept in the custody of said clerk and shall be open to the inspection of any taxpayer of said district.

Board to report, etc.

(§203.) SEC. 7. The said board shall be the board of school inspectors for said district and shall, as such, report to the clerk of the county in which such township is located, and shall have all the powers and perform all the duties now enjoyed and performed by boards of school inspectors; and the president of said board shall perform all the duties required by law of the chairman of the board of school inspectors, and the board of school inspectors for such township is hereby abolished except as its powers are vested in said board of education.

Powers of board, etc.

(§204.) SEC. 8. The board of education of said district shall have power and authority to designate and purchase schoolhouse sites, erect buildings and furnish the same, employ legally qualified teachers, provide books for district library, make by-laws relative to taking the census of all children in said district between the ages of five and twenty years, and to make all necessary reports and transmit the same to the proper officers, as designated by law, so that the district may be entitled to its proportion of the primary school fund: and said board shall have authority to make all needful regulations and by-laws relative to visitation of schools; relative to the length of time school shall be kept, which shall not be less than three months in each year; relative to the employment of teachers duly and legally qualified; relative to the regulations of schools and the books to be used therein; and generally to do all things needful and desirable for the maintenance, prosperity, and success of the schools of said district, and the promotion of a thorough education of the children thereof.

Treasurer to apply for moneys.

It shall be the duty of the treasurer of said board to apply for and receive from the township treasurer or other officer

holding the same, all moneys appropriated for primary
school and district library of said district.

(§205.) SEC. 9. At each annual township meeting held
in said township, the qualified electors present shall determine the amount of money to be raised by tax for all
school purposes for the ensuing year: *Provided,* That in
case the electors at any annual township meeting shall
neglect or refuse to determine the amount to be raised
as aforesaid, then the board of education shall determine
the same at any regular meeting thereof, which amount
the township clerk shall, within sixty days thereafter, certify to the supervisor of the township, who shall spread
the same upon the regular tax roll of said township, and
the same shall be levied, collected, and returned in the
same manner as other township taxes: *Provided,* That for
purchasing school lots and for erecting schoolhouses, no
greater sum than three mills' on the dollar of all the taxable valuation of the real and personal property in said
township shall be levied in any one year. *(margin: Tax for school purposes. Proviso. Idem.)*

(§206.) SEC. 10. All taxes assessed within said township
for school purposes shall be set forth in the assessment
roll of said township, in a separate column, apart and distinct from all other township taxes. *(margin: Of assessment roll.)*

(§207.) SEC. 11. The treasurer of the township shall at
any time, at the written request of said board of education, report to said board the amount of school money in
his hands, and shall, on the order of the president of said
board of education, pay to the treasurer of said board all
such money, taking his receipt therefor, and also a duplicate receipt which he shall file with the clerk of said
board. *(margin: Treasurer to report, etc.)*

(§208.) SEC. 12. The said board shall annually, prior to
the first day of April in each year, make a detailed statement of the number of schools in said district, the number of teachers employed, and the number of pupils
instructed therein during the preceding year, and the
expenditures of said board for all purposes, and also the
resources and liabilities of said district, which report or
statement shall be entered at length in the record of said
board and shall be publicly read by the president of said
board or, in his absence, by the clerk thereof, to the
electors of said township at their annual meeting on the
first Monday of April thereafter, at the hour of twelve
o'clock, noon. *(margin: Board to make statement, etc.)*

(§209.) SEC. 13. All school property, both real and personal, within the limits of a township incorporated as
aforesaid, shall, by force of this act become the property
of the public schools of such township and all debts and
liabilities of the primary school district of said township
as they existed prior to its incorporation under the provisions of this act, shall become the debts and liabilities
of said public schools of the township so incorporated. *(margin: Disposition of school property.)*

Of moneys raised by tax. (§210.) SEC. 14. All money raised or being raised by tax, or accrued or accruing to the school districts of said township as organized under the primary school laws of this State, shall hereby become the money of the public school of the township; and no tax heretofore ordered, assessed, or levied for school purposes in said township or other proceedings, shall be invalidated or affected by means of this act.

Compensation of board, etc. (§211.) SEC. 15. The compensation of the members of the board of education shall be one dollar and fifty cents for each day's actual service rendered for said district; and the clerk and treasurer of said board shall receive such compensation for their services as the board may determine, not exceeding fifty dollars each per annum.

When township is divided, etc. (§212.) SEC. 16. When any township district shall be divided into two or more townships, the existing board of trustees shall continue to act for all the townships, until the same have been organized and township boards of trustees duly elected and qualified therein. Immediately after such organization, the township boards of each of the townships shall meet in joint session and direct an appraisal of all the school property of the former township to be made. When such appraisal has been made, Alteration of township, etc. said township boards shall make an equitable division of the existing assets and liabilities of the school district of such former township, basing their apportionment upon the amount of taxable property in the township divided, as shown by the last assessment roll of such former township. When a township district shall be altered in its limits by annexing a portion of its territory to another township or townships, the township board of each of the townships shall, immediately after such alteration, meet in joint session and make an equitable division of the assets and liabilities of the school district of the township from which the territory has been detached, basing their division upon the amount of taxable property, as the same shall appear upon the last assessment roll of such township.

CHAPTER XXVI.

[Act No. 119, Public Acts of 1891.]

* INTRODUCTION OF THE KINDERGARTEN.

Duty of district board. (§213.) SECTION 1. In addition to the duties imposed by law upon the district board of every school district in this State, they shall also be empowered to provide a suitable room or apartment for kindergarten work, and to supply their district respectively with the necessary apparatus and

---

* This law permits the introduction of the kindergarten method, but does not make it mandatory.

appliances for the instruction of children in what is known as the kindergarten method.

(§214.) SEC. 2. In the employment of teachers it shall be competent for such district board to require qualifications for instruction of children in kindergarten methods; and the district board may provide by contract with the teacher for such instruction, specifying the hours and times therefor under such rules as the district board may prescribe. *Qualifications of teachers, etc.*

(§215.) SEC. 3. All children residing within the district between the ages of four and seven shall be entitled to instructions in the kindergarten department of such district school. *What children entitled to Instruction.*

(§216.) SEC. 4. The powers and duties herein imposed or conferred upon the district shall also be and the same are hereby imposed and conferred upon the school trustees or board of education or other body, by whatever name known, managing or controlling the public schools in each city and village of this State; and this act is hereby made applicable to every public school organized by special act or by charter as fully as if they were named herein. *Act to apply to certain other schools.*

CHAPTER XXVII.

[Act No. 144, Public Acts of 1891.]

UNIVERSITY DIPLOMAS AND CERTIFICATES.

(§217.) SECTION 1. The faculty of the department of literature, science, and the arts, of the University of Michigan, shall give to every person receiving a bachelor's, master's, or doctor's degree, and also a teacher's diploma for work done in the science and the arts of teaching, from said university, a certificate, which shall serve as a legal certificate of qualification to teach in any of the schools of this State, when a copy thereof shall have been filed or recorded in the office of the legal examining officer or officers of the county, township, city, or district. Such certificate shall not be liable to be annulled except by the said faculty of the said University; but its effect may be suspended in any county, township, city, or district, and the holder thereof may be stricken from the list of qualified teachers in such county, township, city, or district, by the legal examining officer or officers of the said county, township, city. or district for any cause and in the same manner that such examining officer or officers may be by law authorized to revoke certificates given by himself or themselves, and such suspension shall continue in force until revoked by the authority suspending it. *University may issue certificate to teach, etc. See §§ 130, 166, 169.* *Of annulling certificate, etc.*

CHAPTER XXVIII.

[Act No. 136, Public Acts of 1893.]

COLLEGE DIPLOMAS AND CERTIFICATES.

Certificates to graduates of certain colleges. See §§ 130, 167, 234.

(§218.) SECTION 1. The State Board of Education is hereby empowered and shall grant teachers' certificates without examination to any person who has received a bachelor's, master's, or doctor's degree from any college in this State having a course of study actually taught in such college, of not less than four years, in addition to the preparatory work necessary for admission to the University of Michigan, upon the recommendation from the faculty of such college, stating that in their judgment the applicant is entitled to receive such certificate; and in addition thereto, a course in the science and art of teaching of at least one college year of five and a half hours per week, which shall have been approved by said board of education, which course shall have been taken by such person who shall have received a diploma therefor, and shall include a thorough examination of the applicant by the college granting such diploma, as to qualification and fitness for teaching: *Provided*, That if said person furnishes to said board satisfactory proof of having successfully taught for three years in the schools of this State, said certificate shall be a life certificate. If such proof is not furnished said board, then such certificate shall be for four years only, and a life certificate may at any time thereafter be issued by said board upon the filing of such proof. Such certificate shall entitle the holder to teach in any of the schools of this State without examination, provided a copy of the same shall have been filed or recorded in the office of the legal examining officer or officers of the county, city, township, or district in which said person is to teach, and shall be annulled only by the State Board of Education, and by it only for cause.

Certificate for four years.

Life certificate.

Board of Education to decide upon college course.

(§219.) SEC. 2. It shall be the duty of the said Board of Education to carefully examine any course of study in the science and art of teaching that may be submitted to it by the trustees of any college and, if satisfactory, to furnish such trustees with a written certificate approving the same.

(§220.) SEC. 3. If at any time the said Board of Education shall conclude that any college the graduates of which may desire to receive such certificate, is not giving such instruction in the science and art of teaching and in the other branches as shall be approved by said board, then said board shall so determine by a formal resolution, and shall give notice thereof to the trustees of such college; and thereafter no teachers' certificate shall be given by said board to the graduate of such college until said board shall be satisfied that proper instruction in the science and art of teaching and in other branches is given by such college, and shall certify such fact to the trustees of such college.

CHAPTER XXIX.

[Act No. 146, Public Acts of 1895.

(§221.) SECTION 1. *The People of the State of Michigan enact,* That there shall be taught in every year in every public school in Michigan, the principal modes by which each of the dangerous communicable diseases are spread, and the best methods for the restriction and prevention of each such disease. The State Board of Health shall annually send to the public school superintendents and teachers throughout this State, printed data and statements which shall enable them to comply with this act. School boards are hereby required to direct such superintendents and teachers to give oral and blackboard instruction, using the data and statements supplied by the State Board of Health.

(§222.) SEC. 2. Neglect or refusal on the part of any superintendent or teacher to comply with the provisions of this law, shall be considered a sufficient cause for dismissal from the school by the school board. Any school board neglecting or refusing to comply with any of the provisions of this act, shall be subject to fine or forfeiture the same as for neglect of any other duty pertaining to their office. This act shall apply to all schools in this State, including schools in cities and villages, whether incorporated under special charter or under the general laws.

CHAPTER XXX.

[Act No. 101, Public Acts of 1895.]

EXAMINATION FOR ADMISSION TO AGRICULTURAL COLLEGE.

(§223.) SECTION 1. *The People of the State of Michigan enact,* That it shall be the duty of the State Superintendent of Public Instruction to secure, at least twice each year, from the president of the Michigan Agricultural College, a set of examination questions in all the studies required for admission to said college. It shall also be the duty of the State Superintendent of Public Instruction to send a printed list of said examination questions to each county commissioner of schools.

(§224.) SEC. 2. It shall be the duty of each county commissioner of schools to give public notice of this examination at the time of all regular teachers' examina-

Conduct of examination.

tions, and to submit the questions aforesaid to any candidate who may desire to enter the Agricultural College. The examination shall be conducted in the same manner as are the regular teachers' examinations of the county. The work of each and every candidate, together with the name and address, shall be forwarded by the commissioner within five days from the date of the examination, to the president of the college, who shall examine and grade the answers and report to the candidate within five days of the receipt of the paper, the result of the examination. A standard, of seventy per cent in each branch will admit to freshman class of the college without further examination.

CHAPTER XXXI.

[Act No. 56, Public Acts of 1895.]

PURCHASE OF UNITED STATES FLAGS.

Size of flag.

(§225.) SECTION 1. *The People of the State of Michigan enact,* That the board of education or the board of school trustees in the several cities, townships, villages and school districts of this State, shall purchase a United States flag of a size not less than four feet, two inches by eight feet, and made of good flag bunting "A," flag staff, and the necessary appliances therefor, and shall display said flag upon or near the public school building during school hours and at such other times as to the said boards may seem proper; and that the necessary funds to defray the expenses to be incurred herein shall be assessed and collected in the same manner as moneys for public school purposes are assessed and collected by law.

NOTE.

APPORTIONMENT OF SURPLUS DOG TAX TO SCHOOL DISTRICT.

Under the provisions of act No. 198, public acts of 1877, as amended by act No. 283 of the public acts of 1881, it is required that in all the townships and cities of the State there shall annually be levied and collected a tax of one dollar upon every male dog and of three dollars upon every female dog. The money thus obtained is to constitute a fund in the several townships and cities for the payment of damages sustained by owners of sheep by reason of having such sheep killed or wounded by dogs. Section six of the law referred to provides that, "If money remains of such fund after satisfactory payment of all claims aforesaid in any one year, over and above the sum of one hundred dollars, it shall be apportioned among

the several school districts of such township or city in
proportion to the number of children therein of school
age." The apportionment must be based upon the whole
number of children of school age residing in the township, and include all districts whether lying wholly or
partly in such township. In case of a fractional district
in which the schoolhouse is situated in a different township, the money belonging to such district must be paid
over to the treasurer of the township in which the schoolhouse is situated, and by that treasurer paid to the district in the same way as in the case of the one-mill and
other taxes.

Act 141 of the Public Acts of 1891 repeals Act number
214, Public Acts of 1889, providing that, if in any city and
any township or part of township adjoining thereto (the
same being within one county) any money remains in the
fund for payment of losses by killing of sheep by dogs
"after the payment of the orders payable out of the same,
and the amount of said money shall exceed the sum of two
hundred dollars, the sum in excess of two hundred dollars
shall be apportioned by said county treasurer to the said
township, or part of township, and said city, in proportion
to the amount contributed to said fund during the preceding year; and the amount so apportioned to any said township, or part of township or said city, shall be respectively
apportioned among the several school districts of said township, or part of township, and said city, in proportion to
the number of children therein of school age." The dis-
tribution of the surplus will hereafter be made in accordance with the provisions of section 6 of Act No. 198, Public Acts of 1877, as amended by Act No. 283 of the Public
Acts of 1881.

11

APPENDIX A.

DIGEST OF DECISIONS OF THE SUPREME COURT.

I.

TOWNSHIP BOARD OF SCHOOL INSPECTORS.

¶1. The statutory notice of meetings by inspectors must be given, stating the object of the meeting; and no business at a meeting inconsistent with the notice is lawful. *Passage v. School Inspectors of Williamstown*, 19 Mich., 330.

¶2. The township board of school inspectors have no power to dissolve a school district erected by special act of the legislature, and to set back the territory into the districts from which it was taken. *School District v. Dean*, 17 Mich., 223.

¶3. On the erection and organization of a new township, the inspectors of such township may sever its territory from the school district within which it was formerly embraced; and there is no general provision of law which charges the property within the new township with the obligation to pay any debts created for school purposes which existed at the time of the erection of the new township. *School District No. 1 of Portage v. Ryan*, 19 Mich., 203.

¶4. *Mandamus* will not be granted to disturb an apportionment made by the township board of school inspectors between different districts, acquiesced in for several years and which, if the court could change it, has no proof that it ought to. *School District No. 3 of Riverside Township v. the Township of Riverside*, 67 Mich., 404.

II.

APPEALS FROM ACTION OF SCHOOL INSPECTORS.

¶5. Under the statute providing for appeals from the board of school inspectors to the township board, the approval of the appeal bond is essential to complete an appeal; and the fact that the bond was presented to the clerk of the board of inspectors, who refused to approve it because it was not witnessed, even though the objection be a frivolous one made in bad faith and for vexation, will not render the bond sufficient without

ı n approval, since, under the statute, it may be approved also by any jus-
·ice of the township. *Clement v. Everest*, 29 Mich., 19.

¶6. The validity of the action of school inspectors in changing the
boundaries of school districts, is not affected by the fact that the inspectors
were interested parties as taxpayers and residents; the disabling doctrine
has no application to those administrative acts which are public and not
with or between private parties. *Ibid.*

¶7. The regularity of the action of school inspectors in creating or
hanging school districts, will not be inquired into in a collateral proceed-
ng; their action is the exercise of a public discretionary power which can
only be reviewed, if at all, by some direct appellate process authorized by
aw and operating upon the proceedings themselves to affirm, reverse, or
hange them. *Ibid.*

¶8. Parties appealing under the statute from the action of school
nspectors in arranging school districts, to the township board, thereby
waive those questions which require judicial review and submit themselves
to the discretion of that body; and a *certiorari* to the township board does
not open for review the doings of the inspectors. *Brody v. Township
Board of Penn.*, 32 Mich., 272.

¶9. It was never intended that a court should exercise any of these
powers of discretionary administration; and when, on such appeal, the
township board acted within its jurisdiction, its discretion cannot be
reviewed by the courts; and if it did not, and its acts were void, then under
the statute the action of the inspectors, after ten days, is equally intact
and beyond disturbance. *Ibid.*

¶10. Where, however, the township board acting without authority,
reverses the action of the inspectors, their doings may be overturned; but
an order of the board affirming the action of the inspectors, whether
properly or improperly, only leaves such action where it would have been
without such interference. *Ibid.*

¶11. A township board has jurisdiction of appeals from decisions of the
board of school inspectors, fixing the amount to be paid by an old school
district to a new one, where the latter comprises part of the same territory
and the former retains the school property. *School District No. 5 of Pine
Township v. Wilcox*, 48 Mich., 404.

III.

TOWNSHIP BOARD.

¶12. An application to a township board to remove the moderator of a
school district, on the ground that he persistently refuses to countersign
an order drawn by the director of the district on the assessor, involves an
inquiry in which the payee named in the order is an interested party.
Stockwell v. Township Board of White Lake, 22 Mich., 341.

¶13. A proceeding before the township board to remove an officer of a
school district, is in the nature of a judicial investigation; and when one
of the board is interested in the subject of the complaint and the presence
of such member is essential to the quorum, the proceedings are void. *Ibid.*

¶14. When either of the members of the township board is interested
in the subject for consideration, he is not "competent or able to act," in the
sense of the statute; and such incompetency will justify the calling in
of one of the remaining justices. *Ibid.*

¶15. Every special tribunal appointed by law is subject to the maxim that no person can sit in any cause in which he is a party or in which he is interested. *Ibid.*

¶16. The removal of a school district assessor by the township board is reviewable on *certiorari*. *Merrick v. Township Board*, 41 Mich., 630.

¶17. Costs awarded by the supreme court in a proceeding by *certiorari* against persons composing a township board, to review their official acts, are to be collected like township charges and not by execution against the officers personally. *Stockwell v. Township Board of White Lake*, 22 Mich., 341.

¶18. Proceedings by a township board to remove a school director are not invalidated by the fact that it did not meet to agree on the notice under which the proceedings were taken. *Wenzell v. Township Board of Dorr*, 49 Mich., 25.

¶19. The primary school law does not authorize the township board to remove the moderator for hiring her husband to teach the district school and agreeing to pay him more than is necessary to secure a better teacher. *Hazen v. Town Board of Akron*, 48 Mich., 188.

¶20. In providing that the school director shall keep the necessary schoolhouse furniture in due order and condition, and that his expenses shall be subsequently audited and paid, it is not intended that money must be put into his hands beforehand. *Township Board of Hamtramck v. Holihan*, 46 Mich., 127.

¶21. The township board is exclusive judge of the facts on which it is authorized to remove a school director, and its proceedings can only be reviewed by the circuit and supreme courts on questions of law. *Ibid.*

¶22. Proceedings by a township board to remove a school director cannot properly be taken until the action of the proper authorities has been invoked by complaint of some definite violation of duty; but where the plaintiff admits the charges set up against him and expressly desires the board to act on them without further delay, he cannot afterwards complain that they did so. *Geddes v. Township of Thomastown*, 46 Mich., 316.

¶23. The action of a township board in removing a school director is final, unless speedily brought up for review. *Ibid.*

¶24. The wilful refusal of a school director to sign a contract made with a teacher, or to accept and file it, or draw orders for the teacher's pay while it is pending, and his obstinate neglect to furnish necessary schoolhouse supplies, may be taken into account in proceedings for his removal. *Ibid.*

IV.

ORGANIZATION OF SCHOOL DISTRICTS.

¶25. There should be some special and extraordinary reason to justify interference by *quo warranto* with the organization of a school district, as the statutes provide a speedier remedy by an appeal from the inspectors to the township board. *Lord v. Every*, 338 Mich., 405.

¶26. When a school district has enjoyed its franchises for five years, during most of which time proceedings to enquire into the validity of the organization had been pending by *quo warranto* and writ of error,

i istead of the speedier statutory process of appeal, the supreme court
eclined to review its organization on technicalities. *Ibid.*

¶27. The legal organization of a school district actually exercising its
corporate powers, cannot be collaterally questioned in contesting a title
ased on a school tax *Stockle et al. v. Silsbee,* 41 Mich., 615.

¶28. A *certiorari* to review proceedings whereby a new school district
as been created out of old districts, must be applied for before the
istrict has been organized and assumed the functions of a corporation;
fter that time the proper course is to take measures to try the legality
if its corporate existence by *quo warranto,* or other direct proceeding
gainst the alleged corporation or its officers. *Fractional School District
No. 1 of Owosso, etc., v. School Inspectors of Owosso, etc.,* 27 Mich., 3.

¶29. *Certiorari* addressed to the assessor of a school district is wholly
insuited as a remedy to test the legal organization and existence of
he district, as the errors, if any there are, lie back of any action of
he assessor and are to be found in the action of the township
authorities. *Jaquith v. Hale,* 31 Mich., 430.

¶30. It has always been the policy of the Michigan school laws that
no primary school district should contain more than nine sections of
land. *Simpkins et al. v. School District No. 1 of Michigamme et al.,*
45 Mich., 559.

¶31. Township school inspectors cannot enlarge a graded school district by adding unorganized territory, though they may, with the consent
of the trustees, transfer to its jurisdiction territory previously organized
into primary districts. *Ibid.*

¶32. Injunction lies to restrain the sale for school taxes, of lands
unlawfully included within the taxing district. *Ibid.*

¶33. A writ of *certiorari* to bring up proceedings for the formation
of a school district will not be sustained, if, after its issue and without
good reason, it has been allowed to sleep until the organization has
been completed, a tax voted, and contract made for building a schoolhouse, and interests established which cannot be overturned without
public inconvenience and injury and individual damage. *Parman v.
Board of School Inspectors,* 49 Mich., 63.

¶34. Where *certiorari* issues to bring up proceedings for the formation of a school district, the papers on which it was allowed must be
served with it. *Ibid.*

¶35. Where there has been actual notice of proposed proceedings by
joint boards for the formation of a new school district out of several
old ones, mere informalities in the issue of such notice are not jurisdictional defects, nor is the fact that it covers territory not actually
taken. *Ibid.*

¶36. The statutory requirement for notice of the meeting of a township board of school inspectors to alter the boundaries of a school
district, is jurisdictional; and proof of posting of such notice should be
filed with the clerk of the board, before any action is taken. *Coulter
et al. v. Board of School Inspectors of Grant and Arthur Townships,*
59 Mich., 391.

¶37. In the absence of the consent of the owners of lands which have
been taxed for building a schoolhouse, within three years last preceding
the date of their proposed transfer to another district, such transfer is
illegal; and the fact that the detached territory was not at the same
time attached to another district will not legalize such transfer. *Ibid.*

¶38. The statutory requirement for notice of the meeting of a township board of school inspectors to alter the boundaries of a district, is jurisdictional; and until such notice has been given and proof of posting made, as required by law, the inspectors have no power to act. *Fractional School District No. 3 of Martin, Watson, and Wayland Townships v. Boards of School Inspectors of said Townships*, 63 Mich., 611.

¶39. Where a *de facto* school district has exercised its franchises and privileges for over two years, it is presumed to have been legally organized, and it is too late to litigate that question in law or equity. *School District No. 3 of Everett Township v. School District No. 1 of Wilcox Township*, 63 Mich., 51.

¶40. The statutory provision requiring the town clerk to give notice of every meeting of the board of school inspectors of his township existing prior to the 1881 amendment, was imperative, and the apportionment by the inspectors of the valuation of school property on the formation of a new district, at a meeting held without such notice, was void; and a bill in equity will lie in the name of the old district to enjoin the assessment and collection of a tax to satisfy the amount so apportioned as its share of such valuation. *Ibid.*

¶41. A township board of school inspectors may, under one notice and at one meeting, by separate action, detach lands from separate school districts and attach them to one district. *Doxey v. The Township Board of School Inspectors of Martin Township*, 67 Mich., 601.

¶42. Where the action of a board of school inspectors in detaching territory from a district without the consent of a majority of the resident taxpayers and attaching it to another district, left land enough in the former for school purposes, they may afterwards consolidate such remaining territory, with the consent of its remaining taxpayers, with any other district which gives a like consent. *Ibid.*

¶43. At a school meeting to vote on the question of dissolving the district, 18 votes were cast in favor of the proposition and 9 against it. Every person present who possessed the qualifications of a voter at any school meeting was allowed to vote, without reference to sex, or whether or not he or she was a resident taxpayer. Ten or more persons who were not resident taxpayers voted, and some of the legal taxpayers did not vote, and some were not present. *Held*, that the consent of a majority of the resident taxpayers had not been obtained as required by Howell's Statutes, §5041. *Briggs v. Borden et al. School Inspectors*, 38 N. W. Rep., 712.

¶44. A bill will lie, at the suit of a resident taxpayer, to restrain the board of school inspectors from selling a schoolhouse and site, furniture, etc., under color of a void attempt to dissolve the district to which such schoolhouse, etc., belongs. *Ibid.*

¶45. Under Howell's Statutes §5041 providing that school districts cannot be divided or consolidated without the consent of a majority of the resident taxpayers of each district, a return by the board of school inspectors stating that the persons consenting are a majority of the resident taxpayers of the districts, is conclusive as to such fact, though the consent filed by the districts does not state that the persons are a majority. *Gentle v. Board of School Inspectors of Colfax Township*, 40, N. W. Rep., 928.

¶46. Proceedings for organizing a new school district, taken without giving the full ten days' notice required by Howell's Statutes §5040, are not rendered valid by filing of a consent by a majority of the citizens of each district affected, such consent being required by §5041, as the notice is a jurisdictional requirement and the minority have a right to be heard and a right to the full notice required. *Ibid.*

¶47. *Quo warranto* is the proper remedy to determine the legal existence of a school district, and the right of particular persons to exercise the offices of moderator, assessor, and director. *People ex rel., Roser et al., v. Gartland Moderator et al.*, 42 N. W. Rep., 687.

¶48. Under Howell's Statutes §5033 providing that no school district shall contain more, than nine sections of land, a district containing five full sections and eight fractional sections, the whole not exceeding in quantity of land nine full sections, is legal. *Ibid*

¶49. The statutory provision concerning the election of school district officers by ballot is mandatory; but where such officers have been unanimously elected by *vice voce* vote at a regular meeting, no other persons claim to have been elected, and they are qualified and are acting, they will not be ousted by *quo warranto*. *Ibid.*

V.

DISTRICT MONEYS, WARRANTS, AND ORDERS.

¶50. An action for money had and received will lie in favor of a school district to recover district moneys received by its assessor, and which after expiration of his term of office he refuses on demand to pay over to his successor, and an action upon the assessor's bond is not the exclusive remedy; the bond is required as additional security, but it does not supersede the officer's individual responsibility. *Mason v. Fractional School District No. 1 of Scio and Webster*, 34 Mich., 228.

¶51. An assessor cannot lawfully withhold the district funds in his hands, when the same are properly demanded by his successor a fortnight after the latter has been regularly elected and has accepted and qualified, upon any claim that he is entitled to be first personally notified officially of such election and acceptance; he is chargeable with notice of these facts without any personal certification thereof. *Ibid.*

¶52. An official treasurer cannot defend an action to make him turn over to his successor the funds in his official custody, upon any questions of the regularity of the proceedings whereby the funds came into his possession. *Ibid*

¶53. The assessor of a school district is the lawful treasurer and depository of school district funds, and all moneys must pass through his hands and be paid out by him on proper orders. *School District No. 9 of Midland v. School District No. 5 of Midland*, 40 Mich., 551.

¶54. A showing of a want of funds is a complete answer to an application for *mandamus* to require an assessor of a school district to pay an order drawn on him in favor of a school teacher. *Allen v. Frink*, 32 Mich., 96.

¶55. It is not necessarily the duty of the moderator of a school district to countersign an order upon the assessor drawn by the director. He has a right to satisfy himself that the claim for which it was drawn is a valid one, and that it was drawn by the director in the proper performance of his duty. *Stockwell v. Township Board of White Lake*, 22 Mich., 341.

¶56. The disbursement of all school moneys is required by the statute to be made by orders drawn on the assessor by the director and countersigned by the moderator; and all moneys belonging to the district in the town treasurer's hands are required to be paid to the assessor on warrants drawn by the director and countersigned by the moderator. The assessor is made treasurer of the district, and required to hold all district moneys until properly drawn out by warrant. It is made the express duty of the director to draw and sign warrants upon the township treasurer, payable to the assessor, for all moneys raised for district purposes or apportioned to the district by the township clerk, and present them to the moderator to be signed; and it is made the duty of the moderator to countersign such warrants. *Burns v. Bender*, 36 Mich., 195.

¶57. District moneys in the hands of the township treasurer are not subject to be applied to any district purpose, except through the hands of the assessor. And the duty of suing to thus transfer them into the custody of the assessor, if qualified, is laid on the director; and the duty of procuring this transfer within some reasonable time is not discretionary, but absolute. The moderator is bound under ordinary circumstances to countersign all orders of the director for that purpose; and if he refuses in a proper case to do so, *mandamus* will lie to compel him. *Ibid.*

¶58. The statute making it the duty of the director to present the warrant to the moderator for signature, he may properly be a relator to obtain it by compulsion of law, when refused. He is the proper custodian of the completed warrant, for the purpose of delivery to the assessor. *Ibid.*

¶59. The query is suggested, whether the assessor would not also be a competent relator. *Ibid.*

¶60. The town treasurer has no authority to make payments of district moneys, even to the assessor, except upon the warrant prescribed by statute; and no payment not authorized by warrant is a valid official payment, such as to preclude the district from holding him responsible for moneys lawfully in his hands. Payments made otherwise than in the prescribed mode, are made in his own wrong and cannot diminish the fund for which he is responsible. *Ibid.*

¶61. Respondent occupying the double position of moderator and town treasurer, is not thereby authorized to set up his previous illegal disbursements of the district moneys as treasurer as an excuse for not doing his duty as moderator; his double functions will not relieve him in one capacity from doing his duty in another. *Ibid.*

¶62. Warrants drawn by the officers of school districts upon the township treasurer for school moneys are not negotiable, and the treasurer is under no obligation to pay them except to the district assessor. *Fox v. Shipman*, 19 Mich., 218.

¶63. An order drawn upon the township treasurer by the director and countersigned by the moderator of a school district, payable to A, or bearer, is void upon its face. The director has no power to draw any order on the township treasurer for any money of the district in his hands, payable to any one but the district assessor, who is the disbursing officer of the district. *Fractional School District No. 4 of Macomb and Chesterfield v. Mallary*, 23 Mich., 111.

¶64: The statute expressly requiring the township treasurer to pay the amount of taxes raised for school purposes to the order of the school district officers, his liability therefor is distinct from his ordinary liability for township moneys, and cannot be released or in any way affected by the action of the township board. *Jones v. Wright*, 34 Mich., 371.

¶65. A township treasurer has no right to receive for school moneys anything which the law has not authorized to be so received, and if he chooses to do so and to receipt for the taxes, he must make good the amount. *Ibid.*

¶66. A town treasurer can pay school moneys only to the school district assessor, and then only on the warrant of the proper district officers. *School District No. 9 of Midland v. School District No. 5 of Midland*, 40 Mich., 551.

¶67. A school district at an annual meeting may lawfully recognize and pay equitable claims, even though they are not strictly legal demands, against it. *Stockdale v. School District No. 2 of Wayland et al.*, 47 Mich., 226.

¶68. A vote to issue school district bonds in settlement of a demand, if in excess of the limit fixed by law, may be sustained up to the legal limit. *Ibid.*

¶69. A corporate act which can only be taken by a two-thirds vote, cannot be rescinded by a bare majority. *Ibid.*

¶70. School orders, payable to bearer, when sold without indorsement at a discount, and it not appearing that the vendor was asked or made any representations as to their character or consideration, it was held that in the absence of false representations or of fraud, the purchasers took them for what they were worth and had no cause of action against the vendor. *White et al. v. Robinson*, 50 Mich., 73.

¶71. A *mandamus* will lie to compel a township treasurer to pay to the assessor of a school district so much of the money in his hands as is covered by the warrant of the director of the district, drawn in favor of the assessor and in proper form, even though it does not specify a precise sum, but is for all such money in his hands as was raised for the purposes of the school district and belonged thereto. *Bryant v. Moore*, 50 Mich., 225.

¶72. The custodian of public funds is bound to make payments on a proper warrant to the extent of the moneys lawfully in his hands and cannot refuse on the ground that his right to the custody of the remainder is disputed. *Ibid.*

¶73. *Mandamus* to compel the payment of money may be granted so far as concerns a portion of the demand, while as to the rest the application is dismissed. *Ibid.*

¶74. When the moderator and assessor of a school district are sued upon an order signed by them, a finding that it was signed on a false and fraudulent statement that the school director approved and would sign it, and on condition that it should be of no force unless he did sign it, and the farther finding that there was no purpose to contract except for the district, defeats an action thereon in the absence of any showing of subsequent action creating contract relations, or of any action by defendants taken with a knowledge of the facts and estopping them personally. *Kane v. Stowe*, 50 Mich., 317.

¶75. *Mandamus* to compel a school district assessor to pay a school order was allowed where the court was satisfied there was no valid defense. *Martin v. Tripp*, 51 Mich., 184.

¶76. Interest from the time of demand may be allowed in granting *mandamus* for the payment of a school order, when it is such a settled demand as would sustain a recovery of interest at law. *Ibid.*

¶77. *Mandamus* will lie on relation of a school district assessor to compel the clerk of a township to which the district formerly belonged, to certify to the supervisor of the township to which it now belongs, the amount ascertained by the school inspectors as due to the new district from what remained of the old district out of which it was erected. *Ramsey v. Clerk of Everett Township*, 52 Mich., 344.

¶78. A town treasurer refusing to pay a warrant drawn in favor of the assessor, whose official character is not questioned, on the ground that the moderator, who has been recognized as such by the other district officers, is not a legal officer, assumes a serious responsibility. The court issued a *mandamus* requiring the town treasurer to pay the order. *School District No. 8 of Tallmadge Township v. Root, Town Treasurer*, 61 Mich., 373.

VI.

TEACHERS' CONTRACTS AND CERTIFICATES.

¶79. When a contract for hiring a teacher has been signed by the director of the school district and by the teacher, and the moderator writes upon it "approved," and subscribes it as moderator, such approval and signature will be treated as in legal effect a signature of the contract by such moderator. *Everett v. Fractional School District No. 2 of Cannon*, 30 Mich., 249.

¶80. The provision of the statute that the contract for hiring a school teacher shall require the teacher to keep a correct list of the pupils and the age of each attending the school, etc., imposes the duty upon the teacher of keeping such list; and this becomes in legal effect a part of his contract, whether the written contract expressly stipulates for it or not. Ibid.

¶81. The provision of the statute requiring the keeping of a list of pupils, etc., to be inserted in the contract is merely directory and does not render invalid a contract from which such requirement has been omitted, provided it be good in other respects and entered into in good faith. *Ibid.*

¶82. A school district is a municipal corporation and cannot be garnisheed, even by its own consent, unless the debtor also consents. *School District No 4 of Marathon v. Gage*, 39 Mich., 484.

¶83. It is against public policy to allow the wages of persons in public employments to be reached by garnishment. *Ibid.*

¶84. School management should always conform to those decent usages which recognize the propriety of omitting to hold public exercises on recognized holidays; and it is not lawful to impose forfeitures or deductions for such proper suspension of labor. All contracts for teaching during periods mentioned must be construed of necessity as subject to such days of vacation, and there can be no penalty laid upon such observances, in the way of forfeitures or deductions of wages. *School District No. 4 of Marathon v. Gage*, 39 Mich., 484. [NOTE.—The legal holidays established by statute are New Year's day (January 1), Washington's birthday (February 22), Decoration day (May 30), Independence day (July 4), Christmas day (December 25), and any day appointed by the president or governor as a day of fasting and prayer or of general thanksgiving. Whenever a legal holiday falls on Sunday, the Monday next succeeding is to be observed instead. *Act No. 124, Laws of 1865, as amended by Act No. 163, Laws of 1875, and by Act No. 208, Laws of 1881.*]

¶ 85. If a teacher is employed for a definite time, and, during the period of his employment, the district officers close the schools on account of the prevalence of contagious diseases, and keep them closed for a time, and the teacher continues ready to perform his contract, he is entitled to full wages during such period. The act of God is not an excuse for non-performance of a contract, unless it renders performance impossible; if it merely makes it difficult and inexpedient, it is not sufficient. Although under such circumstances it is eminently prudent to dismiss school, yet this affords no reason why the misfortune of the district should be visited upon the teacher. *Dewey v. Union School District of Alpena*, 43 Mich., 480.

¶ 86. The statute empowers the board of trustees of a graded school district to employ all teachers necessary, and what teachers are necessary is left to be decided by the sound discretion of the trustees. The making of a contract with a teacher is within the authority of a board of trustees, and, when made, neither the trustees nor the voters at an annual meeting have power to impair its obligation. *Tappan v. School District No 1 of Carrollton*, 44 Mich., 500.

¶ 87. In a suit by a teacher on a contract, the plaintiff is not bound to produce the contract as proof of her certificate of qualification, and it is not error to allow her to give parol proof that she has one. *School District No. 1 of Manistee Township v. Cook*, 47 Mich., 112.

¶ 88. In an action by a teacher on a contract, where it was alleged as error that the contract was allowed in evidence without proof that those who acted for the school district in making it were not authorized, it was held that this allegation did not sufficiently present the objection that the officers of the district were not competent to bind it by a contract extending beyond the current year, especially as there was evidence that the officers were in possession and presumptively competent, and there was no evidence that they were not authorized to employ teachers. *Ibid.*

¶ 89. A school teacher cannot be lawfully employed, excepting at a meeting of the board. *Hazen v. Lerche*, 47 Mich., 626.

¶ 90. A contract with a teacher, if signed by a majority of the board, is presumptively valid on its face and admissable in evidence without further proof. The payment by the assessor without objection, of orders drawn on him by the director and moderator for salary of teacher, estops the district from denying validity of contract under which such services were rendered, and amounts to a ratification of the contract; and direct proceedings by the district board are not essential to such ratification. *Crane v. School District No. 6 of Bennington Township*, 61 Mich., 299.

¶ 91. A teacher's contract is sufficiently executed, if signed by the director and assessor. Simultaneous signing is not necessary. *Halloway v. School District No. 9 of Ogden Township*, 62 Mich., 153.

¶ 92. School district officers should know under what authority a teacher assumes to act, and cannot by failing to hold meetings, set up their own wrong as a defense to an honest claim. A contract signed by the required number of officers, under which the teacher is permitted to teach, with knowledge of the entire board, will be presumed valid. A contract valid on its face and fully performed, with acquiescence of all concerned, cannot be repudiated. *Ibid.*

¶ 93. Although Howell's Statutes, §4969, declares that a certificate from the State Normal School shall serve as a certificate of legal qualification to teach when filed in the county, city, township, or district; failure to file it until after making a contract to teach is no defense to an action for salary earned after it was filed. *Smith v. School District No. 2 of Pleasant Plains*, 39 N. W. Rep., 567.

¶ 94. The general policy of the school law is that schools shall be taught by qualified teachers, but necessities may arise where this cannot be done. A district may be unable to find a qualified teacher. Where the employment of an unqualified teacher is a necessity, the school district is authorized to employ one who has not the proper certificate, if the school board are satisfied that the teacher is otherwise qualified, and to pay such teacher out of the moneys belonging to the district. But the primary school moneys and mill tax cannot be applied to that purpose. *State ex rel. Hale v. Risley, Moderator*, 37 N. W. Rep., 570.

¶ 95. Under Howell's Statutes, §5154, which provides that the secretary of the board of school examiners shall have power to grant special certificates of qualification to teachers which shall not continue in force beyond the next public examination by the board, the secretary has no power four days after such examination, to grant a special certificate to a person who had been teaching under a special certificate granted by the secretary, but who failed to pass the public examination. *Lee v. School District No. 2 of Alcona Township*, 38 N. W. Rep., 867.

¶ 96. The fact that a third person, at a public examination of teachers, acted with a majority of the board of examiners in conducting the examination, does not invalidate the proceedings; and a person who failed to pass cannot complain where it does not appear that such third person had anything to do with her failure to get a certificate. *Ibid.*

VII.

LIABILITIES OF DISTRICTS.

¶ 97. The director of a school district is not legally entitled to compensation from the district for his services. *Hinman v. School District No. 1*, 4 Mich., 168. [NOTE.—The law is since changed so as to authorize compensation to be voted by the district. *General School Laws of 1889*, §27.]

¶ 98. Where two districts are united under the statute, the new district is alone liable for all the former debts of each; and a judgment afterwards rendered against one of the former districts is a nullity. *Brewer v. Palmer*, 13 Mich., 104.

¶ 99. Charts or cards containing the multiplication table, practical forms of business contract, and also brief mention of prominent historical events, and designed for use in school rooms, are held not to be necessary appendages for the schoolhouse, within the meaning of the statute, such as the director is required to provide. *Gibson v. School District No. 5 of Vevay*, 36 Mich., 404.

¶ 100. There was no such necessity for the purchase of these charts as would bring the case within the principles of *School District v. Snell* (see ¶ 103), 24 Mich., 350. *Ibid.*

¶ 101. The purchase of these charts by the director, without instruction from the district board, being unauthorized and void as to the district, his retention of them, and occasionally placing them in the schoolhouse, could not operate as a ratification by the district of his unauthorized purchase. *Ibid.*

ARNING

¶ 102. Orders due from one district to another are not enforceable by *mandamus* at the suit of one to whom they have been assigned. *Maltz v. Board of Education*, 41 Mich., 547.

¶ 103. Where the officers of a school district purchased for the district a set of bound books and some blanks, suitable for the purposes of the district, at their fair value, and while the district was not properly supplied with such material, in the absence of any showing that the discretion of such officers was abused or exceeded, the district is liable. *School District No. 4 of Easton v. Snell*, 24 Mich., 350.

¶ 104. One school district that has wrongfully received money belonging to another cannot in an action by the latter to recover it, require any strict proof of the regularity of the proceedings authorizing it to be collected. *School District No. 9 of Midland v. School District No. 5 of Midland*, 40 Mich., 551.

¶ 105. Where a school district is parceled out among three other existing districts, the latter cannot be held jointly liable for a debt of the former district; whatever they are bound to pay must be a several, and not a joint, obligation. *Halbert v. School Dists., etc.*, 36 Mich., 421.

¶ 106. The statute having confided the management of suits brought against a school district to the assessor when no other direction has been given by the voters in district meeting, the moderator and director, though constituting a majority of the district board, have no authority to take the defense of a suit from the assessor; the control of suits is not among the powers or duties confined by the statutes to the district board. *School District No. 4 of Rush v. Wing*, 30 Mich., 351.

¶ 107. The suggestion that the action of the assessor in this case was such as to be evidence of an adverse interest is disregarded; such a suggestion might be made in any case where the assessor had refused to yield his legal authority to another. *Ibid.*

¶ 108. A judgment for costs against the district on the dismissal of an appeal taken in the name of the district by the director, without the authority or assent of the assessor, on the ground that the district had not appealed, is held to be erroneous. *Ibid.*

¶ 109. Costs are not awarded against the school district in this court, on a writ of error brought without authority of the assessor, to review such dismissal. *Ibid.*

¶ 110. A *mandamus* will lie to compel a school district to pay orders issued by it, even though the district has since been subdivided, where statutory provision for distributing the original liability has not been carried out. *Turnbull v. Board of Education*, 45 Mich., 496.

¶ 111. Interest upon orders issued by a school district is denied upon granting a mandamus to compel their payment, if no authority has been given to impose it. *Ibid.*

VIII.

TUITION OF NON-RESIDENT PUPILS.

¶ 112. Before any action can be maintained under the statutes, for the tuition of non-resident pupils, the district board must first fix and determine the rate of tuition of such pupils, and this should be by resolution of the board, properly recorded by the director in the records of the district; and the fact that such action has been taken; cannot be shown by parol, if objected to.   *Thompson v. School District No. 6 of Crockery*, 25 Mich., 483.

IX.

ADMISSION OF COLORED CHILDREN TO SCHOOL.

¶ 113.   The amendment to the primary school law of 1867—Laws of 1867, vol. 1, p. 42 [*General School Laws of 1889*, § 45]—giving equal rights in the schools to all residents, is applicable to the city of Detroit, and precludes the board of education of that city from excluding a child from any public school on the ground of color. *People v. Board of Education*, 18 Mich., 400.

X.

SCHOOL SITES AND SCHOOLHOUSES.

¶ 114.   Notice of a meeting of the board of school inspectors to change a schoolhouse site is necessary. *Andress v. School Inspectors of Williamstown*, 19 Mich., 333.   (See ¶ 1 preceding.)

¶ 115.   The board of inspectors have no power to change a schoolhouse site on a written request of a majority of qualified voters of the district, except in cases where the site has been fixed by them because the inhabitants were unable to agree upon a site. *Ibid.*

¶ 116.   The jurisdiction to condemn lands for a schoolhouse site is invoked by presenting to the proper officer a petition designating the site and showing disagreement with the owner as to compensation for it. *Smith v. School District No. 2. of Milton*, 40 Mich., 143.

¶ 117.   In proceedings to condemn land for a schoolhouse site, the circuit judge is not required to act in preference to a circuit court commissioner. *Ibid.*

¶ 118.   When the owner of land that is sought for a schoolhouse site is represented at the proceedings to condemn it, he is deemed to waive objection to jurors, if he does not challenge them at the time. *Ibid.*

¶ 119.   When the petition, notice, *venire*, finding, and commissioner's certificate in proceedings to condemn land for a schoolhouse site are regular on their face and show full compliance with statutory requirements, the proceedings are presumed regular; and if the parties interested were represented and omit, on filing the proceedings, to make a· sworn showing to the circuit court of any other defects, such as an omission to designate the site to the jury, they cannot rely on it thereafter. *Ibid.*

¶ 120.   A school district contracting for the building of schoolhouse within a stated time, is bound to furnish a suitable site therefor within such reasonable time that the constructors shall not be delayed on their part. *Todd et al. v. School District No. 1 of Greenwood*, 40 Mich., 294.

¶ 121.   Under a contract for the construction of a school building which provides that the work shall be "executed in the best and most workmanlike manner and agreeably to such directions as may be given from time to time" by the architect or his assistant [the local superintendent of the work employed by the district], "and to his full and entire satisfaction without reference thereon to any other person," [it was held] that all claims for alterations or extras were to be judged of, determined, and adjusted "solely by the superintendent," and that payment should be made on the certificate of the architect or superintendent, partly on monthly estimates, from time to time, and the balance on completion of the building; whatever passed under the inspection of the superintendent as the work progressed, and was in good faith approved by him, expressly or by implication, was not open to objection on the part of the district afterwards; and the certificate of the architect was not a condition precedent to the right of the contractor to recover for the work so approved. *Wildey v. Fractional School District No. 1 of Paw Paw and Antwerp*, 25 Mich., 419.

¶ 122. Variances from such a contract which have been treated at the time as immaterial by both parties will not afterwards be held to be departures from the contract; and what was regarded at the time as substantial compliance with its terms, constitutes a performance in law. *Ibid.*

¶ 123. Intentional departures from such contract, made without the consent, express or implied, of the district officers, architect, or superintendent and in disregard of their directions, would not bar a recovery for other portions of the work which were duly approved; but the district would have a right to insist on the proper changes in the work to make it conform to the contract, and to recover any damages sustained by the failure. *Ibid.*

¶ 124. The mere fact of taking possession and occupying the building by the district for their schools, after the time when, by the contract, it was to be completed, would not, of itself, constitute an acceptance which should bar any claim on the part of the district to insist upon a rectification of any faults, or the payment of any damages they may have suffered by the failure in strict compliance; but the fact of making payments afterward without objection, the manner of taking possession, and whether with or without objection to any variation, would have an important bearing on the question of fact, whether any rights were intentionally waived, or whether there was a purpose to accept the building as completed in substantial compliance with the contract. *Ibid.*

¶ 125. *Mandamus* will not lie to compel a circuit judge to overrule his finding that the proceedings [of] taking for the condemnation of a site for a schoolhouse were irregular, and to compel him to enter judgment for the amount found due. *School District No. 5 of the Township of Delhi v. The Circuit Judge for Ingham County*, 49 Mich., 432.

¶ 126. Proceedings to condemn land for a schoolhouse site will be quashed, if there is no lawful designation thereof shown by the records. *Heck v. School District No. 2 of Essex*, 49 Mich., 551.

¶ 127. The school law (Act 164 of 1881) permits land to be condemned for school purposes only when a site has been lawfully determined, and it confines the power of the township inspectors to determine the site to cases where the inhabitants themselves cannot do it; and it seems that more than one site cannot be designated except by the inhabitants. *Ibid.*

¶ 129. The justice to whom a petition for the condemnation of land for a schoolhouse site is presented, is not empowered to hear evidence or pass on any of the merits. *Ibid.*

¶ 130. Where proceedings to condemn land for a schoolhouse site are brought before a jury, proof of a legal selection of a site must be made to them, and without it they cannot find it to be necessary to condemn it. *Ibid.*

¶ 131. A lease to a school district, to hold the property "during the time it is used for school purposes," is a lease in perpetuity at the will of the

lessee; and, as the lessee is a corporation and words of inheritance are not
required, the lease, if a present consideration is paid, really operates as a
bargain and sale, and conveys a base or determinable fee. This is sufficient
to satisfy the provisions of the school law, which requires a title in fee or a
lease for ninety-nine years, where land is to be secured for erecting a stone
or brick schoolhouse. *School District No. 5 of Delhi v. Everett*, 52 Mich.,
314.

¶ 132. After the lapse of a dozen years it is too late to disturb the title
to a schoolhouse site by mere questions of regularity in the proceedings to
designate it. *Ibid.*

¶ 133. A *surety* on a bond given to secure the performance of a contract
for building a schoolhouse, cannot recover of the trustees of the district
for moneys due him for materials furnished in the erection of the building,
by reason of their failure to require the contractor to execute the statutory
bond provided for by act No. 94, Laws of 1883. *Owen v. Hill et al.*, 67
Mich., 43.

¶ 134. Whether such trustees are liable *in any event* for such neglect of
duty, query,—Sherwood and Champlin, J. J., holding them so liable, and
Campbell, C. J., and Morse, J., reserving their opinion on the subject.
Ibid.

XI.

GRADED AND HIGH SCHOOLS.

¶ 135. The right of school authorities in union school districts of this
State to levy taxes upon the general public for the support of high schools,
and by such taxation to make free the instruction of children in other
languages than English, is sustained. *Stuart v. School District No. 1 of
Kalamazoo*, 30 Mich., 69.

¶ 136. A school district which has assumed to possess and exercise all
the rights and franchises of a regularly organized corporation for thirteen
years, with entire acquiescence of everybody, is not liable to have the regularity of its organization or of the legislation under which it acted, called
in question thereafter, in a merely private and collateral suit. *Ibid.*

¶ 137. Whether or not the statute of limitations applies in terms to a
case where it is not so much the organization of the school district that is
questioned as its authority to establish a high school and levy taxes therefor, it is strictly applicable in principle. *Ibid.*

¶ 138. The organization claimed and asserted by the district being that
of a union school district, the presumption of organization arising from its
user of corporate power must be that of such an organization as its user
indicates, and whether or not an acquiescence for the statutory period of
two years will raise the presumption of regular organization, one of thirteen years certainly will. *Ibid.*

¶ 139. The State policy of Michigan on the subject of education and of
the territory before the State was organized, beginning in 1817 and continu-
ing down until after the adoption of the present constitution, having been
reviewed and considered, the conclusion is reached that there is nothing in
our State policy or in our constitution or in our laws, restricting the
primary school districts of the State in the branches of knowledge which
their officers may cause to be taught, or the grade of instruction that may
be given, if the voters of the district consent in regular form to bear the

expense and raise the taxes for the purpose or to prevent instruction in the classics and living modern languages in these schools. *Ibid.*

¶ 140. The power to make the appointment of a superintendent of schools in a union school district is one that is incident to the full control which by law the district board has over the schools of the district. *Ibid.*

¶ 141. The degree below, dismissing the bill filed in this case to restrain the collection of such portions of the school taxes assessed against the complainants for the year 1872, as has been voted for the support of the high school in the village of Kalamazoo and for the payment of the salary of the superintendent, is affirmed. *Ibid.*

¶ 142. The board of trustees of a graded school have authority to purchase a piano for the purposes of a high school. *Knabe et al. v. The Board of Education of the City of West Bay City*, 67 Mich., 262.

¶ 143. When the law gives the board of trustees power to prescribe the course of studies, it gives them the authority to provide *means* to carry the power into effect. *Ibid.*

XII.

LIBRARY MONEYS.

¶ 144. The treasurer of the board of school inspectors, and not the township treasurer, is the proper custodian of the township library money; and the latter officer, on proper demand, is bound to pay it over to the former and is not entitled to withhold it until it is drawn by the inspectors as needed for specific appropriations; and *mandamus* will lie to enforce the performance of this duty. *McPharlin v. Mahoney*, 30 Mich., 100.

¶ 145. It is a sufficient ground for an application for *mandamus* to enforce such payment, that the township treasurer, when an order was properly drawn on him by the inspectors for such money, but for an amount slightly in excess of the money in his hands, refused to pay over what he had, not on the ground that the order was too large a sum, but upon the distinct assertion that he was himself the proper custodian of the funds, and was not bound to pay them over, except as they were required by the inspectors for special purposes. *Ibid.*

¶ 146. Under the constitution and statutes, all moneys which are paid into the office of the county treasurer, on account of fines, penalties forfeitures, and recognizances, are to be credited to the library fund, and apportioned and paid over by the treasurer to the proper local officers, without any deduction for expenses, either attending the collection of the particular sums paid in or embracing the general criminal expenses of the county. *Board of Education of Detroit v. Treasurer of Wayne County*, 8 Mich., 392.

XIII.

MISCELLANEOUS.

¶ 147. A communication representing that a certain person was of bad moral character and wholly unfit to teach and have the care of a district school, made to a township superintendent by persons interested in a particular school within its jurisdiction, for the sole purpose of preventing

13

the issue to the person so charged of a license to teach the school, is held to be a privileged communication and not actionable. *Wicman v. Mabee,* 45 Mich., 484.

¶ 148. An action will not lie on a communication relating to personal character, if made in good faith and for an honest purpose by persons concerned, and to the proper person. Nor will it lie when such a communication is untrue, if it is is not maliciously made. *Ibid.*

¶ 149. A school director has authority, in the exercise of a sound discretion, to buy new seats for a schoolhouse under a resolution adopted at the annual meeting of the school district "that the school board fix the schoolhouse ready for the winter term." *McLaren v. Town Board of Akron,* 48 Mich., 189.

¶ 150. Act 164 of 1881, in authorizing the removal of a school district officer for illegally using or disposing of any of the public moneys entrusted to his care, does not cover a charge of conspiring with a woman moderator to hire her husband as teacher and pay him more than was necessary to obtain a good teacher. *Ibid.*

¶ 151. If one of two parties claiming the office of moderator obtains a judgment of ouster against co-claimant and is recognized by the director and assessor, he becomes an incumbent of the office *de facto* and his action will be respected while in office. *School District No. 8 of Tallmadge Township v. Root, Town Treasurer,* 61 Mich., 373.

¶ 152. The practice of taking "informal ballots at regular elections has no legal sanction may mislead voters, and is open to grave abuse and is so held when indulged in at annual school meeting. *Ibid.*

¶ 153. A line fence around the schoolhouse site is a "necessary appendage" within the meaning of the statute. "Appendages," under the school statutes, include fuel, fences, and necessary outhouses. The duty of the director to provide the same is not confined to the school term; they should be on hand when the school opens. It then becomes his duty to keep the same in repair, as also the schoolhouse. *Creager v. School District No. 9 of Wright Township,* 62 Mich., 101.

¶ 154. Direction for the payment of primary school money apportioned by the Superintendent of Public Instruction as between districts, if accompanying the apportionment, cannot be altered or modified by the town clerk. *Moiles, Assessor v. Watson, Treasurer, &c.,* 60 Mich., 415.

¶ 155. Title of *de facto* officer will not be tried on application for *mandamus. Ibid.*

¶ 156. The mother of a child included in the school census of the district, who had resided therein more than three months and was more than twenty-one years of age, was entitled to vote at a school meeting for school trustees, though the constitution of Michigan limits the right of suffrage to males, as the constitutional qualifications do not apply to officers for which the legislature has the right to provide, among which are school trustees. *Belles v. Burr et al.,* 43 N. W. Rep., 24.

(NOTE—This decision does not apply to cities whose charters provide that school officers shall be voted for on the same ballot with other municipal officers at a general election. See *Mudge v. Jones,* 59 Mich., 165.)

¶ 157. A rule by a school board that "pupils who shall in any way deface or injure the school building, outhouses, furniture, maps, or anything else belonging to the school, shall be suspended from school until full satisfaction is made," will not be enforced against a boy who accidentally breaks a window glass. Such a rule will not be sustained where the act was done merely through carelessness or negligence, but it must be wilful or malicious to warrant suspension from school. *Joseph H. Holman v. Trustees of District No. 5, Township of Avon.* (Opinion filed Nov. 8, 1889.)

¶ 158. It is the duty of the moderator of a school district to countersign all proper orders drawn by the director or the district treasurer, and if he refuses to countersign such an order issued in full compliance with the provisions of law, *mandamus* will .lie to compel the performance of such duty. *Montgomery v. State*, 53 N. W. Rep., 586.

¶ 159. A contract of employment of a teacher, entered into on behalf of the district by the director and treasurer, will bind the district, although the moderator was not consulted concerning the employment. *Montgomery v. State*, 53 N. W. Rep., 568.

¶ 160. There is no reason why the school district should be put to the cost of a suit by reason of the refusal of the assessor to discharge a duty which might be compelled by proper proceedings against him. *Phillipps v. School District No. 3*, 79 Mich., 170.

¶ 161. The power to adopt text books is conferred by law, and cannot be affected by any rule of the board fixing a time for the reconsideration of motions and resolutions. *Jones v. Board of Education, Detroit*, 88 Mich., 371.

¶ 162. Howell's Statutes, paragraph 3, section 5073, sub. 6, forbids the purchase by a school director of any charts or apparatus for the school without a vote of the district authorizing same; held, not to allow of any purchase by a director, whether acting singly or with the other directors, unless upon authority of the district. *Western Pub. House v. School District No. 1, Locke*, 53 N. W. Rep., 1103.

¶ 163. A notice of a meeting of the board of school inspectors of a township, which is in fact signed by the township clerk, is a valid notice, whether he describes himself as township clerk or as clerk of the board of school inspectors. *McDonough v. Dewey*, 82 Mich., 309.

¶ 164. A notice of the proposed enlargement of a school district by attaching territory taken from two contiguous districts, which gives the exterior boundaries of the district before and after such enlargement, but which fails to name the contiguous districts, is sufficiently definite and certain and shows upon its face that the two districts are to be affected by the proposed action of the inspectors. *McDonough v. Dewey*, 82 Mich., 309.

¶ 165. No power is now conferred by statute upon the voters at an annual meeting to determine whether the school should be kept by a male or female teacher. *Cleveland v. Amy*, 88 Mich., 377.

¶ 166. While we are not prepared to say that the board has a right arbitrarily to refuse a certificate to one possessing the proper qualifications, we are prepared to say that, if the board should refuse a certificate through a personal prejudice or a wilful intent to injure an applicant, and deprive him or her of earning a livelihood at teaching, such person would have the same remedy as any other person who is injured by the malfeasance of a public officer. The matter of selecting or certifying proper and competent teachers in our schools is one of much importance; and, vested as it is, in a board of school examiners who by personal examination are better qualified to survey and consider all the circumstances which should influence one in forming a judgment, we should hesitate to interfere, and will only do so in a case free from doubt and of a gross perversion of duty. *Sturdevant v. School Examiner, Eaton County*.

¶ 167. Plaintiff held a certificate which expired one month after he began his school *   *   *   * failed to procure a certificate upon two trials. It was his business to quit; and after such failure neither one nor all of the district officers could continue him in the school and bind the district to pay for his services, as it is shown that there was no difficulty in obtaining qualified teachers in that vicinity. *Devoe v. School District No. 3*, 77 Mich., 610.

¶ 168. A high school is not a " college " or university within the meaning of Public Acts 1891, No. 147, which provides that graduates of such institutions shall be eligible to the office of county commissioner of schools. *People v. Howlett*, 53 N. W. Rep., 1100.

¶ 169. Under public acts of 1891, No. 147, making the holding of a first grade certificate as teacher a qualification for the office of county school commissioner, such certificate issued to one after his election, though dated prior thereto, is insufficient. *People v. Howlett*, 53 N. W. Rep., 1100.

¶ 170. A first special grade certificate of qualification as teacher can be granted only after the regular public examination provided for by Public Acts 1887, No. 226, and Public Acts 1891, No. 147. *People v. Howlett*, 53 N. W. Rep., 1100.

¶ 171. Where one disqualified under Public Acts 1891, No. 147, to act as county school commissioner, is elected to that office, a judgment of ouster is proper, though there is no opposing claimant for the office. *People v. Howlett*, 53 N. W. Rep., 1100.

APPENDIX B.

FORMS FOR PROCEEDINGS UNDER THE SCHOOL LAWS.

NOTE.—The following blank forms do not comprise a full set for all purposes under the school laws. All furnished by the Superintendent of Public Instruction, together with such as may be required in proceedings where the services of attorneys are usually employed, and a few for which those published may be readily adapted, are omitted. Officers are advised, when performing any duty to which these forms are applicable, to use them in preference to others, as by this means uniformity of administration is secured, many mistakes will be prevented, and in time that which may now seem complicated and obscure will be more generally understood.

FORM No. 1.

Notice by the Clerk of the Board of Inspectors to a Taxable Inhabitant of a District at the Time of its Formation.

[See Compiler's Sections 9 and 10.]

To A_____ B_____:

SIR—The board of school inspectors of the township of_____have formed a school district in said township, to be known as district No._____, and bounded as follows: [Here insert the description.]

The first meeting of said district will be held at_____on the_____day of_____, 18__, at_____o'clock_____M., and you are instructed to notify every legal voter of said district of the same, at least five days previous to said meeting, either personally or by leaving a written notice at his place of residence. You will indorse on this notice a return, showing each notification, with the date or dates thereof, and deliver the same to the chairman of said meeting.

Dated this_____day of_____, 18_____

(Signed)   C_____ D_____,

                             Clerk of the Board of School Inspectors.

FORM No. 2.

Notice of First Meeting—when made in writing to be left at the house of every legal voter.

[See Compiler's Sections 9, 10, and 24.]

To C_____ D_____:

SIR—School district No.____ of the township of_____, having been formed by the board of school inspectors, you, as a legal voter in said district, are hereby notified that the first meeting thereof will be held at_____, on the_____day of _____, 18____, at____o'clock____M.

Dated this_____day of_____, 18_____.

    (Signed)   A_____ B_____

                                  [The person appointed to give notice.]

FORM No. 3.

Endorsement upon the notice (Form No. 1) by Taxable Inhabitant.

[See Compiler's Sections, 9, 10, 24, and 189.]

I, A_____ B_____, hereby return the within (or annexed) notice, having notified the qualified voters of the district, as follows:

NAMES.	DATE.	HOW NOTIFIED.
A_____ B_____	January 1, 1882_____	Personally.
C_____ D_____	" 1, 1882_____	Written Notice.
E_____ F_____	" 2, 1882_____	Personally.
_____	_____	_____
_____	_____	_____

Dated this_____day of_____, 18____

    (Signed)   A_____ B_____

FORM No. 4.

Notice by township Clerk to Director, of Alteration in District.

[See Compiler's Section 18.]

To the Director of School District No._____, Township of_____:

SIR—At a meeting of the board of school inspectors of the township of _____ held_____, 18____, the boundaries of school district No.____, township of _____, were altered in such manner that the territory of said district now includes the following: [Here insert the description.]

Dated this_____day of_____, 18_____.

    (Signed)   C_____ D_____,

                                  Clerk of the Board of School Inspectors.

FORM NO. 5.

Acceptance of office by District Officers, to be filed with the Director.

[See Compiler's Sections 32, 108, and 140.]

I do hereby accept the office of_____in school district No._____
of the township of_____.
Dated this_____day of_____, 18_____.
(Signed)   A_____ B_____.

FORM NO. 6.

Assessor's Bond.

[See Compiler's Section 52.]

KNOW ALL MEN BY THESE PRESENTS: That we, A_____ B_____, assessor
of school district No._____, township of_____, county of_____,
and State of Michigan, C_____ D_____ and E_____ F_____
[his sureties], are held firmly bound unto said district in the sum of_____
[here insert double the amount expected to come into the assessor's hands] to be paid
to the said district; for the payment of which sum well and truly to be paid we bind
ourselves, our heirs, executors, and administrators, jointly and severally, firmly by
these presents.

The condition of the above obligation is such that, if the said_____
_____assessor as aforesaid, shall faithfully discharge the duties of his office
as assessor of said school district, and shall well and truly pay over to the person or
persons entitled thereto, upon the proper order therefor, all sums of money which
shall come into his hands as assessor of said district, and shall, at the expiration of his
term of office, pay over to his successor in office all moneys remaining in his hands as
assessor aforesaid, and shall deliver to his successor all books and papers appertaining
to his said office, then this obligation shall be void, otherwise of full force and virtue.

Sealed with our seals and dated this_____day of_____18___.

A_____ B_____, [L. S.]
C_____ D_____, [L. S.]
E_____ F_____, [L. S.]

Signed, sealed, and delivered in presence of
_____
_____

We approve the within bond.
(Signed)   G_____ H_____, *Moderator.*
                                       J_____ K_____, *Director.*

FORM NO. 7.

Notice of Annual Meeting.

[See Compiler's Sections 21, 23, and 48.]

NOTICE.—The annual meeting of school district No._____ of the township of_____
_____, for the election of school district officers and for the transaction of such
other business as may lawfully come before it, will be held at_____, on Monday, the_____day of September [or July], 18__, at____o'clock___M.
Dated this_____day of August [or July], 18_____.
(Signed)   A_____ B_____, *Director.*

FORM No. 8.

Request to be made by five Legal Voters of a District to the District Board for a Special Meeting.

(See Compiler's Section 22.)

To the District Board of School District No.____ (or to A_____ B_____, one of the District Board):

The undersigned, legal voters of school district No.____ of the township of_____ _____, request you, in pursuance of section 15 of chapter II. of the general school laws of 1889, to call a special meeting of said district, for the purpose of _____·

Dated this_____day of_____, 18____.
(Signed)

C_____ D_____,
E_____ F_____,
G_____ H_____,
I _____ K____·_____,
L_____ M_____·

FORM No. 9.

Notice of Special Meeting.

[See Compiler's Sections 22 and 23.]

NOTICE—*A special meeting* of the legal voters of school district No._____, in the township of_____, called on the written request of five legal voters [or called by the district board, as the case may be], will be held at_____, on the _____day of_____, 18____, at_____o'clock_____M., for the purpose of [here insert *every object* that is to be brought before the meeting].
(Signed) A_____ B_____, *Director.*

FORM No. 10.

Order upon the Assessor for Moneys to be disbursed by him, with Receipt attached.

[See Compiler's Sections 48 and 52.]

Assessor of School District No.____, Township of_____:

SIR—Pay to_____the sum of_____$\frac{\ }{5\,5}$ dollars out of any moneys in your hands belonging to the [here insert name of fund on which order is drawn, as "teachers' wages," "building," etc.] fund, on account of [here state the object for which the order was drawn.]

Dated this_____day of_____, 18____·
A_____ B_____, *Director.*

[COUNTERSIGNED]
C_____ D_____, *Moderator.*

Received of E_____ F_____, assessor of school district No.____, the amount specified in the above order.
G_____ H_____

FORM No. 11.

Warrant upon Township Treasurer for Moneys belonging to School District.

[See Compiler's Sections 48, 52, and 72.]

Treasurer of the Township of_____:

SIR—Pay to A_____ B_____, assessor of school district No.____ in said

township, the sum of _____ _____dollars, out of [here insert the
particular fund], in your hands belonging to said district.
    Dated at _____ _____ ____, this _____ _____day of ___ ____ _____, 18 ____.
                                    C____ _____ D____ _____, *Director.*
          [Countersigned.]
    E____ ____ .___ F____ ____ ____, *Moderator.*

Form No. 12.

Certificate by District Board to Township Clerk, of District Taxes to be Assessed.

[See Compiler's Section 37.]

Clerk of the Township of ____ ____ _____ :
    The undersigned, district board of school district No. ____ ____, township of ____ _____,
do hereby certify that the following taxes have been voted by the qualified electors of
said district, during the school year last closed, and estimated and voted by the district
board, under the provisions of law, viz.:

For teachers' wages _____	$____ ____	_____
For building purposes _____	_____	_____
For repairs _____	_____	_____
For paying bonded indebtedness _____	_____	_____
For fuel _____	_____	_____
For library _____	_____	_____
For apparatus _____	_____	_____
For incidental expenses _____	_____	_____
For _____	_____	_____
Total _____	$____ ____	_____

    Which amounts you will report to the supervisor to be assessed upon the taxable
property of said district in accordance with the provisions of law.
    Dated at ____ _____, this _____day of ____ _____, 18 ...
                        A____ _____ B____ _____, *Moderator.*
                        C____ _____ D____ _____, *Director.*
                        E____ _____ F____ _____, *Assessor.*

Form No. 13.

Bond to be given by the Chairman of the Board of School Inspectors.

[See Compiler's Section 54.]

    KNOW ALL MEN BY THESE PRESENTS: That we, A _____ B _____, the chairman
of the board of school inspectors of the township of _____, county of ____ _____
and State of Michigan, and C____ ____ D _____ and E _____ F ____ ____ [his sureties]
14

are held and firmly bound unto the said township, in the sum of [here insert the sum of double the amount to come into said chairman's hands, as nearly as the same can be ascertained] for the payment of which sum well and truly to be paid to the said township, we bind ourselves, our heirs, executors, and administrators, jointly and severally, firmly by these presents.   \

The condition of this obligation is such that if A _____ B _____, the chairman of the board of school inspectors, shall faithfully appropriate all moneys that may come into his hands by virtue of his office, then this obligation shall be void; otherwise, of full force and virtue.

Sealed with our seals, and dated this ____ ____ day of ____ ____, 18 __.

A _____ B _____, [L. S.]
C _____ D _____, [L. S.]
E _____ F _____, [L. S.]

Signed, sealed, and delivered in the presence of

____ ____ ____ ____ ____ ____ ____

____ ____ ____ ____ ____ ____ ____

I approve the within bond.
(Signed)   G _____ H _____, *Township Clerk.*

FORM No. 14.

Appointment of District Officers by District Boards.

[See Compiler's Sections 90 and 108.]

The undersigned, members of the district board of school district No. _____, township of _____, do hereby appoint A _____ B _____ [*director, moderator,* or *assessor,* as the case may be] of said district to fill the vacancy created by the [removal, resignation, or death, etc.] of C _____ D _____, the late incumbent.

Dated this _____ day of ____ _____, 18 _____.

E _____ F _____
G _____ H _____

FORM No. 15.

Appointment of District Officers by School Inspectors.

[See Compiler's Sections 30 and 108.]

The undersigned school inspectors of the township of _____, do hereby appoint A _____ B _____ [*director, moderator,* or *assessor* as the case may be] of school district No. _____, in said township, the district board having failed to appoint.

Dated this ____ day of _____, 18 _____.

C _____ D _____,
E _____ F _____,
G _____ H _____,
Board of School Inspectors.

FORM No. 16.

Notice of Meeting of Inspectors.

[See Compiler's Section 15.]

NOTICE.—A meeting of the board of school inspectors of the township of _____ _____, will be held at _____, on the _____ day of _____ 18 ____, at ____ o'clock ____ M., for the purpose of [here insert *every object* that is to be brought before the meeting, and if for the purpose of changing boundaries of districts, state the alterations proposed.]

Dated this_ _ _ _ _ _day of_ _ _ _ _ _ _ _ _ _ _, 18_ _ _ _

A_ _ _ _ _ _ _ _ _ _ B_ _ _ _ _ _ _ _ _ _

Clerk of the Board of School Inspectors.

FORM No. 17.

Certificate to be given to the Director of a School District, by the Board of School Inspectors when they establish a Site.

[See Compiler's Section 89.]

The inhabitants of school district No._ _ _ _ _ _, township of_ _ _ _ _ _ _ _ _ _ _ _ _ _ _ _ _ _, having failed, at a legal meeting, to establish a site for a schoolhouse, the board of school inspectors hereby certify that they have determined that the said site shall be as follows [here insert description.]

Given under our hands this_ _ _ _ _ _ _day of_ _ _ _ _ _ _ _ _ _, 18_ _ _ _ _.

A_ _ _ _ _ _ _ _ _ _ B_ _ _ _ _ _ _ _ _ _,
C_ _ _ _ _ _ _ _ _ _ D_ _ _ _ _ _ _ _ _ _,
E_ _ _ _ _ _ _ _ _ _ F_ _ _ _ _ _ _ _ _ _.

Board of School Inspectors.

FORM No. 18.

Warrant on the Township Treasurer for Library Moneys.

[See compilers Section 115.]

To the Treasurer of the Township of_ _ _ _ _ _ _ _, County of_ _ _ _ _ _ _ _ :

SIR—Pay to_ _ _ _ _ _ _ _ _ _ _ _ _, chairman of the board of school inspectors, the sum of _ _ _ _ _ _ _ _ _ _ _ _ _ _ _ _ _ $\frac{}{}$ dollars, from the library moneys in your hands or to come into your hands, the same being for the support of the library of said township.

Dated at_ _ _ _ _ _ _ _ _ _ _, this_ _ _ _day of_ _ _ _ _ _ _ _, 18_ _ _ _ _.

A_ _ _ _ _ _ _ _ _ _ B_ _ _ _ _ _ _ _ _ _,
C_ _ _ _ _ _ _ _ _ _ D_ _ _ _ _ _ _ _ _ _,
E_ _ _ _ _ _ _ _ _ _ F_ _ _ _ _ _ _ _ _ _.

Township Board of School Inspectors.

REMARK.—In case one or more district libraries are established in a township the library moneys due each districts are payable on the order of the district officer. (See Form No. 11.)

FORM No. 19.

Notice by the Township Treasurer to the Township Clerk of Moneys to be Apportioned to Districts.

[See Compiler's Sections 72 and 73.]

To the Clerk of the township of_ _ _ _ _ _ _ _ _ _ _, County of_ _ _ _ _ _ _ _ _ _ :

SIR—I have now in my hands for apportionment to the several school districts of this township the following moneys:

Primary school interest fund_ _$_ _ _ _ _ _ _
Library moneys received from county treasurer_ _ _ _ _ _ _ _ _ _ _ _ _ _ _ _ _ _ _ _
One-mill tax_ _
Surplus dog tax _
District taxes _
Special funds _

Dated this_ _ _ _ _ _ _day of_ _ _ _ _ _ _ _ _ _ _, 18_ _ _ _ _.

A_ _ _ _ _ _ _ _ _ _ B_ _ _ _ _ _ _ _ _ _,

Township Treasurer.

FORM NO. 20.

Notice by the Township Clerk to the Township Treasurer, of the apportionment of Moneys to Districts.

[See Compiler's Sections 63 and 64.]

To the Treasurer of the Township of _____ ____, County of _____ ____:

SIR—Herewith find a statement of the number of children of school age in each school district of this township, entitled to draw public moneys, and the amount of moneys apportioned to each of said districts:

Districts.	No. of children in district.	Primary school interest fund.	Library moneys.	One-mill tax.	Surplus dog tax.	District taxes.	Special funds.	Total to each district.
District No. 1		$	$	$	$	$	$	$
District No. 2, fr'l								
Total		$	$	$	$	$	$	$

Dated this _____ day of _____, 18_____.

A _____ B _____,
Township Clerk.

FORM No. 21.

Notice by the Township Clerk to Directors, of Moneys belonging to the Districts.

[See Compiler's Section 64.]

A _____ B _____, *Director of School District No. _____, Township of _____:*

SIR—The amount of school moneys apportioned to school district No. _____, township of _____, is as follows:

Primary school interest fund _____$ _____
Library moneys received from county treasurer _____ _____
One-mill tax _____ _____
Surplus dog tax _____ _____
District taxes _____ _____
Special funds _____ _____

Total _____$ _____
Dated this _____ day of _____, 18_____.

A _____ B _____,
Township Clerk.

FORM No. 22.

Certificate by the Township Clerk to the Supervisor, of District Taxes to be Assessed.

[See Compiler's Section 62.]

Supervisor of the Township of _____, County of _____:

SIR—I hereby certify that the following is a correct statement of moneys proposed to be raised by taxation for school purposes in each of the several school districts of this township, as the same appears from the reports of the district boards of the several districts now on file in my office:

DISTRICTS.	For teachers' wages.	For building purposes.	For repairs.	For paying indebtedness.	For fuel.	For library.	For apparatus.	For incidental expenses.	For	Total.
District No. 1	$	$	$	$	$	$	$	$	$	$
District No. 2, fr'l										

Which amounts you will assess upon the taxable property of each of said districts in accordance with the provisions of law.

Dated this.... ....day of............., 18.....

A.... .... D.... ....,
Township Clerk.

FORM NO. 23.

Deed to School District.

[See Compiler's Section 35.]

KNOW ALL MEN BY THESE PRESENTS: That A...... B......., and C...... D......., his wife, of the township of............., county of............., and State of............., party of the first part, for and in consideration of the sum of.... ....$\frac{}{00}$ dollars, to them paid by the district board of school district No............., of the township of ...., county of.... ...., and State of Michigan, the receipt whereof is hereby acknowledged, do hereby grant, bargain, sell, and convey to school district No.... .... aforesaid, the party of the second part, and their assigns forever, the following described parcel of land namely [here insert description]; together with all the privileges and appurtenances thereunto belonging, to have and to hold the same to the said party of the second part and their assigns, forever. And the said party of the first part for themselves, their heirs, executors, and administrators, do covenant, grant, bargain, and agree, to and with the said party of the second part and their assigns, that, at the time of the ensealing and delivery of these presents, they were well seized of the premises above conveyed, as of a good, sure, perfect, absolute, and indefeasible estate of inheritance in the law, in fee simple, and that the said lands and premises are free from all encumbrances whatever; and that the above bargained premises, in the quiet and peaceable possession of the said party of the second part and their assigns, against all and every person or persons lawfully claiming or to claim the whole or any part thereof, they will forever warrant and defend,

In witness whereof, the said A...... B........., and C....... D........, his wife, party of the first part, have hereunto set their hands and seals, this .... day of.... ...., 18.....

A.... .... B.... ...., [SEAL]
C.... .... D.... ....; [SEAL]

Signed, sealed, and delivered in presence of
E.... .... F.... ....,
G.... .... H.... ....

STATE OF.... ...., } ss.
County of.... ....

On this.... ....day of.... ....in the year one thousand eight hundred and ...., before me, I.... .... K.... ...., a.... ...., in and for said county personally appeared.... ...., and.... ...., his wife, to me known

to be the same persons described in and who executed the within instrument, who-
severally acknowledged the same to be their free act and deed.
    Witness my hand and official seal, the day and year last above named.
                                    I____ ____ ____ K_____, [SEAL.]
                                    ____ ____ ____ ____ ____ ____

FORM No. 24.

Lease to School District.

[See Compiler's Section 35.]

    KNOW ALL MEN BY THESE PRESENTS: That A_____ B_____, of the town‾
ship of_____, county of_____, and State of_____, of the first
part, for the consideration herein mentioned, does hereby lease unto school district No.
_____, in the township of_____, county of_____, and State of Mich-
igan, party of the second part, and their assigns, the following parcel of land, to-wit:
[Here insert description] with all the privileges and appurtenances thereunto belonging;
to have and to hold the same for and during the term of_____years from the_____
day of_____, 18____. And the said party of the second part, for themselves and
their assigns, do covenant and agree to pay the said party of the first part, for the said
premises, the annual rent of____ ____dollars.
    In testimony whereof, the said parties have hereunto set their hands and seals, this.
_____day of_____, 18____.

                    A____ _____ B____ _____, [SEAL.]
                                                       Lessor.
                C____ _____ D_____,
                E____ _____ F_____, } [SEAL.]
                G____ _____ H_____,
        *District Board of School District No.*____ *of the aforesaid Township.*
Signed and sealed in the presence of
    I _____ K_____,
    L_____ M_____.

FORM No. 25.

Contract for Building a Schoolhouse.

[See Compiler's Section No. 35.]

    Contract made and entered into between A_____ B_____ of the township of
_____, in the county of_____, and State of Michigan, and C_____ D_____,
E_____ F_____, and G_____ H_____, composing the district board of school
district No.____, of the township of____ _____, in the county of_____, and State of
Michigan, and their successors in office.
    In consideration of the sum of one dollar in hand paid, the receipt whereof is hereby
acknowledged, and of the further sum of_____dollars to be paid as hereinafter
specified, the said A_____ B_____ hereby agrees to build a _____ schoolhouse,
and to furnish the material therefor, according to the plans and specifications for the
erection of said house hereto appended, at such point in said district as said district
board may designate. The said house is to be built of the best material, in a substantial, workmanlike manner, and is to be completed and delivered to the said district
board or their successors in office, free from any lien for work done or material furnished, by the_____day of_____, 18__. And in case the said house is not finished
by the time herein specified, the said A_____ B_____shall forfeit any pay to the
said district board or their successors in office, for the use of said district, the sum of
_____dollars, and shall also be liable for all damages that may result to said
district in consequence of said failure.
    The said district board or their successors in office, in behalf of said district, hereby
agree to pay the said A_____ B_____the sum of_____dollars, when the founda-

tion of said house is finished; and the further sum of___ _____dollars when the walls are up and ready for the roof; and the remaining sum of_____dollars when the said house is finished and delivered as herein stipulated.

It is further agreed that this contract shall not be sub-let, transferred, or assigned without the consent of both parties.

Witness our hands this_____day of_____, 18____.

A_____ B_____,
Contractor.

C_____ D_____,
E_____ F_____,
G_____ H_____,
District Board.

Form No. 26.

Contract between District Board and Teacher.

[See Compiler's Sections 38, 40, 56, 109, and 128.]

It is hereby contracted and agreed between the district board of school district No.____ in the township of_____, county of_____, and State of Michigan, and A_____ B_____, a legally qualified teacher in said township, that the said A_____B_____ shall teach the school of said district for the term of_____months, commencing on the_____day of_____, 18___; and the said A_____ B_____agrees to faithfully keep a correct list of the pupils, and the age of each attending school, and the number of days each pupil is present, and to furnish the director of the district with a correct copy of the same at the close of the school, and to observe and enforce the rules and regulations established by the district board.

The said district board, in behalf of said district, agrees to keep the schoolhouse in good repair, to provide the necessary fuel to keep the schoolhouse in comfortable condition, and to pay said A_____ B_____for the said services as teacher, to be faithfully and truly rendered and performed, the sum of_____dollars per month, the same being the amount of wages above agreed upon, to be paid on or before the_____ day of_____, 18__: *Provided,* That in case said A_____B_____shall be dismissed from school by the district board, for gross immorality, or violation of this contract, or shall permit h___certificate of qualification to expire, or shall have said certificate annulled or suspended by the county board of school examiners or other lawful authority, h____shall not be entitled to any compensation from and after such annulment, suspension, or dismissal.

In witness whereof, we have hereunto subscribed our names, this_____day of _____, 18____.

C_____ D_____,
E_____ F_____, } *District Board.*
G_____ H_____,)
A_____ B_____, *Teacher.*

Form No. 27.

Teacher's General Register.

[See Compiler's Section 40.]

REGISTER of the school taught in District No._____, of the township of_____, in the county of_____, and State of Michigan, for the term commencing on the_____day of_____, 18---, and ending on the_____day of _____, 18---.

NO.	NAME	Age	January 6	January 13	January 20	January 27	February 3	February 10							Total attendance in days	Orthography	Reading	Writing	Arithmetic	Geography	Grammar	U. S. History	Civil Government	Physiology and Hygiene
																ATTENDANCE IN DAYS FOR WEEK COMMENCING				STUDIES PURSUED BY EACH SCHOLAR					
1	A_____ B_____	7	5	3	4	5	2	4							23	*	*		*	*				*
2	C_____ D_____	14	4		5	1	3	5							18	*	*		*		*		*	*
3	E_____ F_____	10	3	4	4	3	5	4							23	*	*		*	*				

I hereby certify that the above is a faithful and correct register of said school.

A------------ B------------, Teacher.

Note.—The above register, properly certified by the teacher, should be filed with the director of the district immediately after the close of the school. Each column under the head of "Attendance in Days" is designed to embrace the number of days present each week, and the sum of days present during the term given in the twentieth column to the right.

The words "for weeks commencing" (in the above form) refer to "January 6" in the left hand column under the head of "Attendance in Days," etc. The star, thus *, denotes the studies pursued by each pupil. To ascertain the average number of days scholars attend school, add together the numbers of days of attendance of all the pupils (as found in twentieth column) and divide this sum by the number of pupils who have attended school.

☞ The teacher should make out this average and indicate it upon the register, for the convenience of the Director.

Under the provisions of §42, the teacher is required to certify in the register, before placing it in the hands of the Director, whether or not instruction has been given in physiology and hygiene, with special reference to the effects of alcohol and narcotics upon the human system, in the school or grade presided over by the teacher.

APPENDIX C.

RULES FOR SCHOOL LIBRARIES.

NOTE.—The following regulations for the management of the school libraries are prepared in accordance with the provisions of Compiler's Sections 3 and 115 of the general school laws. As given these rules are suitable for township libraries; if it be desired to adapt them to the needs of district libraries, a few slight changes which are readily apparent, will be necessary.

1. The librarian shall have charge of the library, and keep a catalog of all the books belonging to the library, in a book to be provided for that purpose.

2. Every volume in the library shall have posted on the inside of the cover a printed label, giving the name of the township, the number of the volume, and the fine for not returning it within the specified time, and for the loss of or injury to any book.

3. Every volume loaned shall be entered by the librarian in a book to be provided for that purpose, by its catalog number, with the day on which it was loaned, the name of the borrower, and the name of the person to whom it is charged (see regulation 5), the date when returned, and condition of the book, and the fine assessed for detention or injury to the book, as in the following form:

Date of Delivery.	No. of book Delivered.	To whom Delivered.	To whom Charged.	When Returned.	Condition when Returned.	Fine for Detention.	Fine for Injury.

4. No person shall be allowed to have more than one volume at a time, or to retain the same longer than two weeks; nor shall any person who has incurred a fine imposed by these regulations, receive a book while such fine remains unpaid.

15

5. Books may be loaned to minors and charged to their parents, guardians, or other persons with whom they reside, who shall be responsible for the books under these regulations.

6. On the election of a librarian, his predecessor shall, within ten days thereafter, deliver to him all the printed and manuscript books, pamphlets, papers, cases, and all other property belonging to the library which was in his custody, for which the librarian shall give him a full receipt, discharging him from all responsibility therefor, except in the case herein provided; and on receiving the library property, the librarian shall carefully examine all books and other property appertaining to the library; and if any loss or injury shall have been sustained, for which a fine has not been imposed by his predecessor, or for which a fine has been imposed but not certified by him to the treasurer of the board of school inspectors, the librarian shall certify the amount thereof to said treasurer, who shall collect the same of such predecessor in the same manner as other fines are collected.

7. In case of vacancy in the office of librarian, the township clerk shall perform the duties of librarian, until the vacancy is filled.

8. If any person having held the office of librarian, shall neglect or refuse to deliver to his successor all the library property, as prescribed in the sixth regulation, the treasurer of the board of school inspectors shall forthwith commence an action in the name of the township for the recovery of the property he shall so neglect or refuse to deliver.

9. On the return of every book to the library, the librarian shall examine it carefully, to ascertain what injury, if any, has been sustained by it, and shall charge the amount of the fine accordingly.

10. The following fines shall be assessed by the librarian as herein provided:

First, For detaining a book beyond two weeks, five cents per week;

Second, For the loss of a volume, the cost of the book; and, if one of a set, an amount sufficient to purchase a new set;

Third, For a leaf of the text torn out or lost, or so soiled as to render it illegible, the cost of the book; and, if one of a set, the cost of a new set;

Fourth, For an injury beyond ordinary wear, an amount proportionate to the injury, to be estimated by the librarian, subject to revision, upon appeal, by the board of school inspectors;

Fifth, Whenever any book shall not be returned within six weeks from the time it was loaned, it shall be deemed to be lost, and the person so detaining it shall be charged with its cost in addition to the weekly fine for detention, up to the time such charge is made. But if the book be finally returned, the charge for loss shall be remitted; and the fine for not returning the book shall be levied up to the time of such return: *Provided,* That in no case shall the amount of weekly fines exceed double the cost of the book.

11. On the third Monday of August, November, February, and May, and also immediately before he vacates his office, the librarian shall report to the treasurer of the board of school inspectors, the name of every person liable for fines and the amount each of such persons is liable to pay; and said treasurer shall immediately proceed to collect the same and, if

not paid, he shall forthwith bring an action in the name of the township for the recovery thereof.

12. The library fines collected shall first be applied to the replacing of lost volumes, binding pamphlets, and rebinding such books as may require it.

13. On the first Monday of September in each year, the librarian shall report to the township board of school inspectors as follows:

First, The number of volumes in the library;

Second, The number of volumes purchased during the year;

Third, The number of volumes presented during the year;

Fourth, The number of volumes loaned during the year [counting each volume once for each time it is loaned];

Fifth, The amount of fines assessed;

Sixth, Such other items as the board of school inspectors may require for their annual report to the Superintendent of Public Instruction.

INDEX.

INDEX.

     16

Page

17

18

19